HEADLANDS

Headlands

THE MARIN COAST AT THE GOLDEN GATE

MILES DeCOSTER

·

MARK KLETT

·

MIKE MANDEL

·

PAUL METCALF

·

LARRY SULTAN

Published for Headlands Center for the Arts by

The University of New Mexico Press

ALBUQUERQUE

Library of Congress Cataloging in Publication Data

Headlands: the Marin coast at the Golden Gate / Miles DeCoster . . .
    [et al.].
        p.   cm.
    Bibliography: p.
    ISBN 0-8263-1151-2. — ISBN 0-8263-1152-0 (pbk.)
    1. Marin Peninsula (Calif.)—Description and travel.
I. DeCoster, Miles. II. Headlands Center for the Arts.
979.4'62—dc20   89-32247
                                                      CIP

iv   Contemporary photographs copyright © 1989 by Mark Klett.
Text copyright © 1989 by Paul Metcalf.

First edition.

    Thanks are due to the following, for permission to quote from
published work:

    The University of California Press, excerpts from *Weather of the
San Francisco Bay Region*, by Harold Gilliam, © 1962 by the Regents
of the University of California.
    Harold Gilliam, excerpts from *San Francisco Bay*, Garden City,
New York, 1957.
    American Geophysical Union, excerpts from *A Streetcar to
Subduction, and Other Plate Tectonic Trips by Public Transport in San
Francisco*, by Clyde Wahrhaftig, © 1984 by American Geophysical
Union, Washington, D.C.
    Clyde Wahrhaftig, written communication, 1987 and 1988,
excerpts from other publications, as listed in the bibliography.

C O N T E N T S

THE publication of *Headlands: The Marin Coast at the Golden Gate* marks a time of transition for the Marin Headlands. After 100 years of military occupation, obscure and off limits to the public, the Marin Headlands, under the stewardship of the Golden Gate National Recreation Area, are emerging into the light of public use. In spite of their proximity to San Francisco (a ten-minute drive), it is just now toward the end of the 1980s that the headlands are becoming more than a well-kept local secret and are attracting visitors from around the world. *Headlands* is a portrait of this place — hills, cliffs, beaches, and coves unwittingly protected against the advances of commercial development by the army. The headlands are rich in historical significance, natural beauty, and environmental phenomena, and countless incidents of irony, juxtaposition, and camouflage. This book is a portrait of the quiet turnings and sudden grandeur of a wild place. It also tracks the process of discovery by five artists who began their explorations of the headlands in the fall of 1987. It is our hope that, like the headlands, the book will have well-traversed areas, some looked at only from a distance, as well as some hidden valleys and coves.

This book was one of the first projects commissioned by Headlands Center for the Arts. It embodies the mission of the center, which is to support artists in their research and explorations of the Marin Headlands and to make their interpretations available to the public. The center enables artists to use its extraordinary location and facilities (eight buildings in an abandoned army fort) as resources for exploring new ways of working and new ways of interacting with the public. It serves as a laboratory where artists are invited to research and develop ideas that explore the relationship between place and the creative process. Artists from around the country and abroad in the visual arts, literary arts, performing arts, and media arts are offered housing and work space at the center and encouraged to collaborate with each other and with other professionals in the headlands The center works as a partner with the National Park Service, restoring its historic structures and offering extensive arts programs to the public.

Headlands was conceived in 1985 by Helen Brunner, Don Russell, and Jock Reynolds as a project that would provide a public service and one that would offer artists an unusual opportunity. Since the material was so complex and layered, a collaboration was envisioned from the start. A team of artists from around the country was selected.

They had not worked together in the past, but all had dealt with historical source material in a contemporary format and could each provide the different elements necessary to develop a book. Paul Metcalf from Chester, Massachusetts, developed the text, both by compiling existing material and by finding links to create a narrative. Mark Klett from Tempe, Arizona, photographed the headlands in their current state and documented contemporary sites from the same vantage points as those found in archival images. Photographers Larry Sultan (Greenbrae, California) and Mike Mandel (Santa Cruz, California) created a portrait of the headlands from existing images found in military files and the National Archives. Miles DeCoster, a book artist from Chicago, refined the assembled material and designed the book. The process has taken two years and has been a collaboration of its own design. All decisions about the direction, form, content were made by all five artists at our various working sessions. Each artist's voice remains clear and recognizable without creating an imbalance in the overall portrait.

The artists and the center are grateful to the following people who made this book possible: National Park Service employees Brian O'Neill, Gordon Chappell, Faith Duncan, Judd Howell, John Martini, Dan Sealy, Terri Thomas, and Warren White who provided invaluable information at every stage of the project. Also thanks to Allen Fish, Carter Faust, Wilma Follette, Colonel Milton B. Halsey, Jack Tracy, Clyde Wahrhaftig, and Elizabeth Poulliot who shared with enthusiasm their extensive knowledge of the Marin Headlands. Thanks are also in order to Colonel Mervyn F. Burke, John Busch, Witten Harris, Colonel Mario G. Paolini, Harry Peterson, Casius Eugene Poole, Willis E. Spitzer, and Kent Williams who provided a vital personal dimension to the historical data in hours of interviews. Suzanne Hellmuth served as the project's Washington, D.C., researcher, spending hours in the files of the National Archives and the Defense Department looking for photographs. (It should be noted that although the army meticulously documented all of its installations and activities throughout its occupation of the area, there is relatively little material on the Marin Headlands in the National Archives. Word has it that there are tens of thousands of photographs that are unavailable for public perusal because there is not the staff to catalogue them.)

We are grateful for the support of the following organizations: National Endowment for the Arts, California Arts Council, Marin Community Foundation, Fleishhacker Foundation, Fireman's Fund Insurance Company Foundation, T. B. Walker Foundation, and Art Matters Inc. They deserve an extra round of thanks because they took a chance on the center in its early and unproven years.

We have enjoyed our relationship with the University of New Mexico Press and our editor, Dana Asbury, who accepted the project as unique and who patiently guided it to publication. We are grateful to the press for maintaining the artists' vision.

Lastly, the artists themselves are to be saluted for their patience in sticking with this project over the years. Their intelligence and humor has guided them through a complicated and difficult process. They struggled with temptations to "smooth out the wrinkles" and become predictable in the effort to be accessible or to accommodate each other. They wrestled with definitions of "guidebook," attempting to balance public expectation with their private mission as artists. Foremost in their minds was the effort to develop a project that was artistically strong and intact and yet of interest to a broad public. The center is proud to offer this guidebook of sorts and hopes it encourages explorations of the Marin Headlands and discoveries even beyond what we have found.

Jennifer Dowley
Executive Director
Headlands Center for the Arts

*Headlands: "a cape; a promontory; a point of land
projecting from the shore into the sea. . . ."*

THE Marin Headlands, a series of coastal hills,
capes, cliffs, coves, and beaches shaping the northern edge of the
entrance to San Francisco Bay, form a landscape that seizes the senses
and urges the curiosity. Comprising 15,000 acres, the headlands were
formerly Indian territory, then a single ranchero, then dairy farms
and military fortifications, once almost a private development, and
they are now public lands: a part of the Golden Gate National Recreation Area.

To create a focus for this book, it was decided at the beginning to
establish arbitrary boundaries. Anchored at one corner by the northern end of the Golden Gate Bridge, the line runs north along the
freeway (California 101), west along the ridge bordering the northern
side of Tennessee Valley, south along the Pacific Ocean to Point
Bonita, and east to the gate, along the coastal entrance to the bay.
This is "our" Marin Headlands.

The land itself, and its uses, are the subject of our work, and, more
than that, the place we honor. From the start, my exposure, as writer,
occurred on four levels, almost simultaneously: the physical experience, by car and on foot, of the land and its constructions; indoctrination by various experts in the many disciplines involved — geology,
archeology, botany, ornithology, civilian and military history, and so
on; interviews with earlier tenants, military and civilian; and finally,
the research, digging into the archival resources.

From the beginning I was struck by the idea of *migrations*. The
land itself, the very rock of the headlands, has moved over a period
of 200 million years from volcanic eruptions in the mid-Pacific. The
weather is a daily, weekly, annual cycle of fog, sun, and rain — sally
and retreat. Overhead, the hawks, the raptors, are in annual migration.
In prehistory the Miwok Indians immigrated from the north; later,
from the south, came the Spanish, and later still, from the Azores,
the Portuguese. The plant life, the vegetation, includes a jumble of
imports or exotics, most notably that Australian immigrant, the
eucalyptus. Finally, the military batteries and missile sites — the most
visible survivors of human occupation — followed an unconscious
migration route, from the narrowest point of the gate, northwestward,
steadily, to Point Bonita and beyond — from the Civil War to after
World War II — each new construction reflecting superior military
technology, and obsolescence of the old.

Larry Sultan likes to think of these *migrations* as *transformations*. They may also be conceived as *layers*. For my purposes, though, I still find the idea of *migration* more dynamic. It is an idea that carries over into the processes of research, and the construction of the text.

Like the chert and basalt of which the headlands rocks consist, the materials, the resources, seemed to emanate from great distances. The Miwok Indians, and later the Russians, came from Siberia, the Spanish from Sonora, the Yankee ships from Boston, and the British from halfway around the world — and all pouring into the Marin Headlands, creating a centripetal intensity, like a whirlpool. This dynamic was reflected in the process of research itself: compared to the older eastern states, California is supposed to be "new," and yet there is an abiding historical concern here; I found the majority of what I sought, some of it what I consider "exotic" material, hidden away in the small town and county libraries of Marin County. (I spent one day in the California Room at the San Francisco Public Library, feeling completely alienated, on the wrong side of the gate. I was not displeased when I found nothing of use.)

There were other resources here at the headlands: the sometimes chaotic Park Service files at the Visitor's Center; the on-site seminars and field trips, conducted by professionals; and an odd meeting of coastal artillery hobbyists that a few of us stumbled into — men who gather from all over the world to relive the glory days of the big guns.

The intensity of this place is further reflected in the jealousies it engenders, jealousies among the experts. There is scarcely an issue here, scarcely a resource text, that does not have its proponents and adversaries. Hence, many a section of the text of this book will be controversial. Where controversy exists, I have made considered judgments, perhaps arbitrary, but following the line that seemed most likely to me. I have generally chosen to *take a position*, rather than skirt the issue and produce a text of blandness.

Exposure to this sort of bubbling conflict, on both major and minor matters, is a sobering experience for a writer of history. But more than that, it is evidence, again, of that centripetal intensity, here in the Marin Headlands.

We, the five collaborators on this book — Miles DeCoster, Mark Klett, Mike Mandel, Larry Sultan, and myself — were, with a couple of exceptions, only somewhat known to one another before the project began. By and large, it has been the book and the place that have brought us together.

Mike: I think the choice [of collaborators] was a good one, because we all have disparate attitudes that we brought to it. We are all different kinds of people.

Although we all had experience of the headlands, only Mark had direct, daily contact — by the nature of his work, shooting on site. For the rest of us, the "thing" we were creating, the book, was a construct, designed from materials in part local and physical, deriving directly from the headlands, and in part removed, found in archives and libraries.

We felt we were five individuals, each determined to secure a working space that would both define and protect his own integrity, and at the same time we surprised one another, more than once, by acts of accommodation.

Was it because beneath each individual temperament lurked "Mr. Nice Guy"? Or were we, consciously or not, restraining our wildest impulses in deference to the collaboration, in which we were determined to serve the abiding hero of this book, the Marin Headlands?

Our first week together was a crash program of indoctrination, with seminars, texts, and field trips.

Larry: Because I didn't photograph here . . . instead gaining a lot of factuality and research . . . all these things seemed like words against the wall. They never really described this place. Going into the archives, collecting material, that's one reality; and then the place, which, to me, is absolutely different. They almost have no relation. I find the place to be almost immutable, unknowable, removed.

Mike: Our researches led us to so many personalities who had invested their own identities in the headlands. There was really very little about the real, visceral rush of the fog, and the space, all the things that Mark got from coming out here to take photographs.

Mark: When I really got into this place was when I left all those seminars, those interpreters behind; when I had the freedom to go out on my own. The explorations: that's what I love. I love going up on Hill 88 and discovering some of those things. I look for them, that's the kind of stuff I look for. I think it's the kind of stuff a lot of people look for.

Larry: For me, what makes this place come alive is an overlay of my own personal memory. The beach, the smell, the mysterious quality of those batteries. . . . I remember going down in the Nike missile base, where there was fear of asbestos, that was the intensity of this place, it was dangerous. It was not only dangerous, it was unpredictable: there were cults, and there was asbestos, and they're equally dangerous — they're both unseen deadly forces, and you don't know where they're going to attack. . . .

The visits to the headlands — four in all — were particularly poignant for me, coming as I did from the East Coast, three thousand miles away, a world apart. Each time there was the anticipation, and then, when I got here, evocations, memories.

Mark: It has to do with a personalization of space, which I think, somehow, this place cultivates.
Larry: How do you get to know a place? What do you learn from a guidebook? We have set out to make a guidebook, our own version of being guides. Each of us in his own way is trying to guide someone through a personalized experience of the Marin Headlands. And I guess I'm concerned about the frailty of this invitation, of being guides.
Mike: But I don't think we are trying to make a guidebook. We're trying to create an evocation.
Mark: And the archives, granted they're an incomplete shard of the place, can nonetheless be an invitation.

The accommodations we made with one another were not compromises. At one point Larry felt that I, as writer, and Miles, as designer, were restraining ourselves, restraining our aesthetics. He felt it was "elegant restraint," and he appreciated it, but he wondered why we did so.

Miles: To do something adequate to the feelings engendered by this place dictated our simple, but subtle, approach. The design reflects the nature of the place, its shifting moods, its textures.
Mark: Part of what we may have called restraint is respect for collaboration; but more important, it's respect for the Marin Headlands.

In a way I think we have created a narrative without a narrator. Text and photographs are their own speakers, their own voices. By the time the book was finally coming together, it had become an entity, almost palpably moving, floating in the space amongst us. It had taken over.

Coming from San Francisco, you will cross the Golden Gate Bridge and turn off the freeway at the Alexander exit. If you come from the north, turn off at Sausalito. In either case, approach the one-way tunnel. If you're lucky, the light will be green; more likely, you'll wait up to six minutes, on red. The six-minute tunnel.

Emerging at the western end, on Bunker Road, you may find the weather altogether different, almost a change in the climate: foggy and cool at one end, sunny and clear at the other. The tunnel is a rite of passage.

Continue west on Bunker Road, past the military housing, past the junction with McCullough Road, crossing what used to be the firing range, and passing the army stables on the left, and you will come to a bushy area, the bushes up close against the guard rail, on your right. Park your car here — there is room to do so, off the road — and find the footpath that penetrates the bushes. You will cross a small stream, where the steelhead used to run, and emerge in a clearing, on Miwok Trail. Turn right, and follow this a short distance to a junction with the Bobcat Trail. Pause a moment. Follow the Bobcat Trail, with your eye, up Gerbode Valley. You will see a clump of tall eucalyptus, isolated, along the trail. This is the site of one of the old dairy ranches, the Silva ranch.

On the hillsides, off the trails, you will occasionally run into daffodils: domestic flowers, house flowers, that have escaped into the wild. Approaching the eucalyptus, you will pass, on the right, the site of the ranch house: a few bricks, some garden flowers, and rose bushes. On your left — these you will have to imagine, there is nothing remaining — were the calf pens, the hay barn, the sheds for the milkers, the milking barn, and the bull pens. Look up to your right, you will see the remains of the old cistern, on the hilltop. Below, near the path, lies an old iron water tank; at the path's edge, the hydrant stands. Off to your left, spreading up the western hillsides, are two fields that were clearly cultivated: one was the hayfield, and on the other the Silvas grew artichokes.

Ambling back to your car, if you are attentive, you may notice an occasional helicopter or other aircraft, but otherwise, there is very little to hear. There may be deer, bobcat, or jack rabbit on the hillsides, and hawks overhead.

The Silva ranch is a quiet domestic pocket in the awesome Marin Headlands — a "home place" — now returning, quietly, to the wild.

Paul Metcalf

MARIN (muh-RIN): The name of a great Miwok Indian chief who fought the Spaniards, was captured, imprisoned, escaped, and continued to terrorize the missions; or the bastard son of a Spanish sailor who escaped from a wrecked galleon, his mother the sailor's native consort; or a simple Indian boatman who crossed the Bay on an armful of bulrushes; or no Indian at all, but a Spanish sailor, "el marinero" ("unlikely Marin was an Indian name . . . in his native language the sound 'r' does not occur"). Legendary Indian chief, skilled sailor, or first one and then the other; Miwok or Spaniard; or no one in particular: there is tradition but no evidence for all and none. . . .

8

● Ship making port before a change of weather.

SOME thirty miles to the west — outliers and guardians of the headlands — stand the Farallons: "small rocky islands in the sea." The earliest Russians on the northwest coast were the *promyshleniks* — Kamchatkan and Siberian fur-hunting privateers. Enslaving the native Aleuts, they occupied the Farallons, built stone huts, set up a base for hunting seals and the sea otter, which they called *bobrimorski* — sea beaver: a shy creature, with eyes "full, black and piercing." Armed with bone-tipped spears, the Aleuts put to sea in their bidarkas, waterproof craft, with the native's outer garment fastened to the craft's sealskin covering — so that native and bidarka, paddling through turbulent waters, appeared as one sea creature. (The Aleut referred to the otter as "my brother" — but, under Russian domination, he seemed to have no compunction against fratricide.) Seated in his bidarka, he waited for hours, perhaps days, for his prey.

There were neither wood nor water on the Farallons, and five or six times a year the Russians would pay the islands a visit to collect skins and refresh supplies. Little wood was needed, though, as cooking was done mostly with oil-soaked bones. For twenty years the hunt continued — until seals and sea otters were virtually exterminated.

Later — between 1850 and 1856—the Faralone Egg Company of San Francisco brought into the city, from the Farallons, between three and four million eggs — eggs of several birds, among them one called the *Foolish Guillemot*.

People who have lived on the islands say that during storms one can hear a kind of moaning noise against the breaking waves. And in the very worst storms, the Farallons are said to shake....

◇　　◇　　◇

... In the forms of arcs and a series of dips and rises ... only to side-skip, arc, dive, and rise again ... another repeating the maneuver, then another, and another ... moving often in a series of long ellipses....

Round and round it goes — a short sweep into the wind and a long one to the leeward — no movement of wings or tail beyond a constant small adjustment of their planes—up, and up, and up ... the tail, in soaring, spread open like a fan ... the wings spread to their greatest extent, the outer primaries curved upward slightly and separated like the fingers of an open hand ... each bird independent of the others, traveling alone ... in silence.

Thus the hawks — ospreys, kites, harriers, accipiters, eagles, falcons — all birds of prey, to be found under the term *raptor* — in annual migration through the Marin Headlands.

Lawrence C. Binford, California Academy of Sciences: "For several years prior to the fall of 1972, I noted raptors migrating past my office window at the east end of Golden Gate Park, San Francisco. ..." Studying the contour maps and following their track, he traced them to the highest hill above Pt. Diablo — Hill 129 — or, in military term, Construction 129, the last of the great coastal artillery batteries in the headlands.

Binford: "On 21 September 1972 ... I visited Pt. Diablo and was rewarded with 162 individuals of 10 species of raptors. ..." Pt. Diablo and Construction 129 were still under military control, and the hilltop was in the line of fire from the rifle range, where practices were regularly held. Not a place from which to observe hawks.

Emanating from as far north as Alaska and northern Canada, following the valleys between mountain ranges, taking advantage of the larger wind patterns, and the local warm air currents — the thermals — that rise from the valley floors along the mountain sides, the migrating hawks find themselves funneled naturally into the Marin Headlands. Disliking open water, they come to 129 with the bay to the east, the ocean to the west, and the San Francisco peninsula little more than a mile ahead. Here the bird hesitates, picks up a thermal rising from the water's edge along the southern slope of 129 — circles, soars, rises, dips and rises, up, up, tail spread, wings extended, to the peak of the current's lift; then, closing tail, tucking wings to body, dives at an angle, conserving body fat and energy for the long trip ahead — dives as though shot from the rifle range at his back — for the San Francisco shore, and the next thermal — to continue the journey southward.

The swainson's hawk, the osprey, and the peregrine falcon may fly as far as Argentina. The swainson's, particularly, arrives in a state of exhaustion, having taken little time to feed along the way. Many of them die at journey's end, or are eaten by predators, or, it is said, by some of the desperate native populace.

Because no records were kept a hundred years ago, it is difficult to determine which species of raptors have adapted the best to man-made changes in the landscape — and which have suffered. The great horned owls and the red-tailed hawks like to nest in that great Australian invader, the eucalyptus tree—so their numbers have no doubt increased. The kestrel has also adapted well. But raptors are at the end of the food chain, and are most vulnerable to chemical contaminants and pollutants. The harriers, the peregrine falcons, the red-shouldered and cooper's hawks have likely all suffered in numbers.

Nevertheless, Pt. Diablo, or Hill 129, or Construction 129, or, as ornithologists now have it, Hawk Hill — is the single major hawk lookout point in all of western North America.

◇　　◇　　◇

According to aboriginal tradition, San Francisco Bay had once been a valley, fertile and beautiful, broken by hills and watered by two rivers.

Or it was an oak grove, with a single river flowing through. In native legend, the name for Golden Gate was *Yulupa*: Sunset Strait.

"Ancestors of the Miwoks and of all the Native Americans . . . were migrating Siberian hunters."

where the sun sleeps. our fathers came thence.

"These early wanderers crossed to Alaska from Asia. . . . "

the earth opened in the west, where its mouth is

" . . . when there was a land bridge across the present Bering Straits."

it would be good to live on the other side

The first peoples to enter what is now California, from the north, arrived some 10,000 years ago. The Miwok, of the Penutian family, were among the several tribes that followed. They settled the Marin area perhaps 5,000 years ago. The Penutians have been linked by some linguists with the Maya.

(The Costanoans, settling the San Francisco peninsula, are known to have had boats that carried them to the Marin shore. According to one theory — "that cannot yet be proven" — they may have occupied some portion of the shore, at least for a time.)

In Miwok legend, there was a mysterious land, far to the north: "*wali-kapa* was a sort of cliff or mountain. Beyond it the young ducks live. They say that on the other side the sky comes way down. It is to the north; it is not reached by a passage that is closed."

Originally, there was neither creation nor creator, although Coyote was a dominant figure. His land lay far to the west, beyond the ocean. He appeared first on the primeval water, followed by his grandson, Chicken hawk, the latter in the form of a feather floating on the water.

When Coyote appeared, the land was covered with water. Coyote shook his *walik* — something like a blanket — to the south, east, north, and west. The water dried and the land appeared.

Coyote tried to regulate the tides, but he had them so low that most of the fish died. Later, he corrected the error, and arranged the tides as they are today.

Coyote was "mean" and "never helped people; he worked by himself. . . . Crab woman did not like him because when he opened his mouth, it had too strong, too bad a smell.

"In the early days, people didn't die. But Coyote wanted to hear people crying after somebody had died. He liked to listen to the noise. I don't remember who was the first to die."

Eventually Coyote returned west, across the ocean, "and built a house over there where the sun sets. He worked for days and could not stop. The top of his house could be seen from the hills there. Coyote didn't like that. He wanted to make smoke. Sometimes he smoked tobacco. He wanted fog or smoke to cover the 'shine' of his house. One day, early in the morning, he smoked. Then he stopped. He made the fog stay, and even when the wind blows, his house is still covered."

When people die, they go to the west, to be with Coyote. "The dead go toward Point Reyes and go down there. They say there is a little chunk of wood there, which they use to make a fire. A piece of rock about two feet long is at the spot where they jump into the ocean and then follow a road back of the breakers."

With a permanent settlement near present-day Sausalito, the Coast Miwok hunted and fished the headlands. But the staple of their diet was acorns — from the tan oak, black oak, and blue oak. "Acorns were gathered in the fall, sometimes with the aid of knocking sticks and often off the ground after the first strong wind of the late fall and early winter." Probably, too, they were found after the grasses were burned.

The acorns were ground to a fine flour, then cleansed of tanic acid through water leaching. "Acorn flour was used to make soups, thick porridges, and, among some groups, even bread. To make mush, acorn flour and water were placed in a water-tight basket in which fire-heated rocks were stirred until the mixture was cooked. Acorn breads were often baked in above-ground or underground ovens. The importance of acorns is signified by the number of foods to which the Indians referred as condiments to acorn dishes. Salmon, deer, fresh berries, dried kelp, a host of herbs and fresh greens. . . . "

Hunting and fishing on the headlands were seasonal. "Some animal foods, such as deer and crab, were available all year. Winter and early spring were times of shortage, when stored dried acorns and seeds, plus kelp . . . were the mainstay. Nevertheless, there were salmon runs; mudhens were available, and in late winter, geese. In spring, small fish stranded at low water in pools on the rocks were collected, and another kelp . . . was eaten. . . . "

"Marine foods were important. Sea mammals were not eaten, but there was heavy reliance on fish. Surf fish were caught in a circular dip net; bay fish, in a seine strung between two tule balsas. Only for bullhead was a line with a gorge used. Steelhead and salmon were taken during the winter runs. . . . Eels were netted or were poisoned. . . . Of shellfish, only mussels and several kinds of clams were important as food."

One elderly informant stated that "bear was scarce; deer not plentiful, but more common than bears; rabbit more prevalent than either; but they 'ate more clams than rabbits.' Bear, elk, and deer were the large game animals; rabbit, cottontail, wood rats, gophers, and squirrels, the small ones. Land birds were trapped or netted, some for food, some for feathers. Aquatic birds were varied and plentiful."

Eagles, buzzards, ravens, owls, and frogs were considered sacred, and were not hunted.

"Sexual abstinence was required several days prior to fishing or hunting, and these activities were suspended during the wife's menstrual period and following the birth of a child. A deer hunter lived on acorn mush and pinole for two days prior to the hunt and ate no saltwater food except kelp."

The archeology indicated that, over a period of unnumbered centuries, "they had achieved something quite rare in human history: a way of life that gave them peace and stability, not just for a generation or two, not just for a century, but probably for thousands of years."

The goal of each successive tribal chief was to not lose ground: to "stay where we are."

When the first Europeans asked them their names, they said *Michako*, meaning, *we are the people*. Over the years this became corrupted to *Miwok*. And over a very few years, at the hands of the restless Europeans and their diseases — the missionaries, the land- and gold-seekers, the epidemics of malaria and small pox — the Miwoks were destroyed.

"By the early 1930s, there were perhaps three individuals predominantly Coast Miwok in blood. . . . Effectively people and culture have disappeared."

◇   ◇   ◇

In the summer of 1597, Sir Frances Drake, coasting northward in vain search for a northwest passage, stood off the Golden Gate, by the Farallons — and the fog was in. His chaplain, Francis Fletcher, made notes:

"Neither could we at any time, in whole fourteene days together, find the aire so clear as to be able to take the height of sunne or starre." And: "We could very well have been contented to have kept about us still our winter clothes."

Fletcher hated the fog, found it "vile, thicke, and impenetrable." He even claimed that "it stank."

In the year 1769 — nearly two centuries after Drake — Gaspar de Portola, first Spanish governor of Alta California, was leading an overland expedition up the coast, when his advance scouts happened to catch a glimpse of a body of water. . . .

Portola's chaplain, Father Crespi, wrote of the sighting: "It is a harbor such that not only the navy of our own most Catholic Majesty but those of all Europe could take shelter in it."

Six years later the Spanish Viceroy Antonio Bucareli sent three ships from Mexico loaded with supplies for a mission, to be erected on the shores of these newfound waters. One of the ships, the *San Carlos* (with a second name, *Golden Fleece*), was under the command of Captain Miguel Manrique, who had orders to explore the harbor seen by Portola's men. But on the voyage north, Manrique became unstable, threatening shipmates with loaded pistols. Judged "not in his right mind," he was replaced by a thirty-year-old junior lieutenant, Juan Manuel de Ayala. In the removal of the pistols, one was accidentally discharged, wounding Ayala in the foot.

Pausing at Monterey, Ayala ordered his men to build a long boat from the trunk of a redwood tree. The boat was completed in two days and placed on board the *San Carlos*.

Early on an August morning in 1775 Ayala recorded sighting the rocky islets "of St. Francis" — the Farallons. The fog had lifted. In the afternoon he reached the entrance to the bay, and had the long boat placed in the water with a crew of ten, to explore the interior waters for a good anchorage.

Night fell and the long boat failed to return. Driven by powerful west winds, with a churning tide ahead, and lighted by a crescent moon, Ayala slid beneath the headlands and into the bay, where the *San Carlos*, or *Golden Fleece*, dropped anchor. The next morning the long boat appeared, its crew having been bedeviled through the night by contrary currents.

Ayala and his men spent forty-four days in the bay exploring, mapping the area, and conversing with the Miwoks.

Jose de Canizares, chief surveyor, left instructions for future mariners: do not sail too close to what later became Lime Point (from the bird lime), or Fort Point — the Marin Headlands.

In the fall of the same year — October 1775 — Don Juan Bautista de Anza, with a party of 240 Sonorans and Sinaloans — trained to

● Presidial pueblo of San Francisco in 1830.

be able to eat almost anything — departed from Tubac in the Sonora desert, to journey by land to San Francisco Bay. They arrived in the spring — March 23, 1776 — and Father Font of the reconnaissance party declared San Francisco was "a marvel of nature, and may be called the port of ports."

Anza selected an inland site for the mission, and a site for the presidio, high above the gate's south shore.

In 1777, Felipe de Neve, Governor of the Californias for Spain, was under strict orders to be on the lookout for Captain Cook's two vessels then roaming the Pacific, and by no means to permit them to enter any California port.

Orders were soon given that *no* foreign ships or foreign visitors were to enter Spanish territory. The less other nations saw of the miles of fertile land, fine harbors, and rich forests (and the thin scattering of Spanish occupants), the better.

As early as 1769, Gaspar de Portola had written from Monterey that "the Russians are about to invade us."

In the sixteenth century Yermak, the Russian robber chief, had crossed the Ural Mountains, and the Russian conquest of Siberia had begun — culminating in Admiral Behring's discovery of northwest America, and most notably, the fur seal. "Starting about the same time, the Russians had crossed and occupied Siberia, had crossed Behring Sea and occupied the American coast and established communications with Asia by a ship built of American timber, before the English moving on the Atlantic coast had yet more than reached the Mississippi River."

The Spanish mission system, pushing northward from Mexico, was in response, in part at least, to the Russian fur hunters, pushing south from Alaska.

(The Russians had designs on the entire California coast, as far south as San Diego; and the Spanish at one time maintained an outpost as far north as Nootka.)

Communications between the two groups were complicated by difficulties with the languages. If a message was unwelcome it was convenient to pretend not to understand it.

In 1789, a new element was introduced:

Governor Fages issued an order to Commandant Jose Arguello at San Francisco: "Should there arrive at the port of San Francisco a ship named *Columbia*, which they say belongs to General Washington of the American states, and which under the command of John

Kendrick sailed from Boston in September 1787 with the design of making discoveries and inspecting the establishments which the Russians have on the northern coasts of this peninsula; — you will take measures to secure the vessel and all the people on board. . . ."

Suspicious as they were of each other, the Russians and Spanish came to be unified in their mistrust of the tricky Yankees shipping out of Boston — the aggressive, antimonarchist Protestants, ruthless and unscrupulous in trade.

Nor were the English forgotten:

In 1792, a ship under command of Captain George Vancouver entered the bay, and Vancouver effectively spied on mission and presidio:

"The [Spanish] soldiers are totally incapable of making any resistance against a foreign invasion, an event which is by no means improbable." They have "2 useless guns." "Why such an extent of territory should have been thus subjugated, and after all the expense that has been bestowed on its colonization turned to no account whatever, is a mystery in the science of state policy not easily to be explained."

Vancouver refused to learn Spanish and persisted in calling California, as far south as San Diego, New Albion.

In 1812 the Russians constructed a substantial settlement on the coast, some sixty miles north of the bay, on a thousand acres, purchased from the Indians. They erected a redwood stockade with blockhouses, gunports, a chapel, barracks, kitchen, warehouses, and jail. The commandant's house was furnished with glass windows, carpets, and a piano. Outside the stockade were wooden huts for the Aleuts, a shipyard, and farm buildings. They planted cereal grains, hemp, tobacco, and garden vegetables. The settlement was named Ross, from "the root of the name Russia, a word extending far back into antiquity. It may have meant little Russian." The Spanish called it *El Fuerto de los Russos*.

From here the Russians sent the Aleuts southward in their bidarkas, to hunt sea otter in the Farallons, along the headlands, and into the bay . . . and the Spanish lacked either guns or boats with which to drive them off. Occasionally, despite their suspicions, the Russians entered into partnership on these ventures with the tricky Yankee traders. And over the years, despite royal orders from Spain, despite language barriers — but because of mutual necessity — an uneasy and generally unrecorded trade developed between Russian and Spaniard. The Russians received fruit seeds, wheat, and livestock for their farm, and in return provided iron and metal goods.

In 1822 Mexico won independence from Spain, and in this unstable political climate, the Russians pressed their adventuring, proposing themselves once more to the Spanish-Mexicans as protectors against the dreaded Yankees.

The Spanish, happy with trading, entertained the Russians at the bay. On one occasion, Governor Sola "arranged a bull and bear fight. Several soldiers borrowed a boat owned by the mission and crossed the Golden Gate to the north shore where they captured two bears. They brought back the smaller one because the larger was too difficult to transport. The fight with the bull was staged on the Beach." The outcome was not recorded. But Kotzebue, the visiting Russian, described the spectacle as "remarkable."

At the height of Russian-Spanish-Yankee partnerships and trade, the Russians nearly gained a foothold on the Marin peninsula, at Sausalito. But the sea otter and fur seal — the basis of Russian wealth — were nearing extinction. At the same time the Russians proved to be miserable farmers. The settlers at Ross were hungry, and poor, as support from St. Petersburg was withdrawn.

In 1841, Ross — land, buildings, furnishings, and livestock — was sold to John Sutter of New Helvetia — on whose land gold was soon to be discovered.

Russian influence receded, and disappeared.

August 2, 1822, the British schooner *Orion* arrived at the bay, and the first mate, one William Anthony Richardson, was sent ashore to secure water, beef, and firewood. Arriving at the presidio, he found an entertainment under way, and the host, Governor de Sola, welcomed the young Englishman. Richardson danced with the governor's daughter, Maria, and, depending on which account you read, he either did or did not make love to her that night. Again, with varying accounts, he may have returned to the ship the next morning, engaged in a furious fight with the captain, and knocked him senseless. In any case, he returned to the presidio, and the *Orion* sailed without him.

De Sola seemed delighted with his new guest — as was his daughter, Maria. In less than a year, Richardson was baptized into the Catholic faith by Padre Jose Altimira, and he became Guillermo Antonio Richardson. In due course he received Mexican citizenship, and in May 1825, celebrated his marriage to Maria.

Besides helping to relieve the boredom at the presidio, Richardson proved a valuable ally to the governor, teaching him new ways to impose levies on visiting ships.

He was described by contemporaries as "a swindler and opportunist" and, conversely, as a man who "had not a single enemy," and was "kind, honest, and generally beloved." Another said that "Richardson was full of Mexican authority and Anglo Saxon enterprise." His son, Steve, asserted that his father "made his way through the world merrily, both with mankind and with womankind" and he "loved a good fight next to making love."

Maria, the patient wife, said "she never understood exactly what he was doing, but since it made him content, she was satisfied."

What he was doing was, among other things, swindling and graft — which, given the time and place, provided him with little distinctive coloring. He rose in local society, was considered a *don* and a *persona de razon* (the latter title applied to anyone who was not an Indian or a peon).

In 1838 Richardson determined to secure his position by taking up ranching, and he applied to the Mexican authorities for a grant of land: some 19,000 acres on the Marin peninsula — from the bay to the ocean, from the headlands to Mount Tamalpais. (Other grants in the area were for as many as 56,000 acres.) The property came to be called Rancho Saucelito (Sah-oo-thay-lee-toh, meaning "little yellow or willow thicket").

Mexican procedures for distributing the California lands were "simple, imprecise, and latent with trouble.

"1. The petitioner 'prayed' for the land, specifying how much he wanted and where it was, submitting a primitive map (*diseño*) showing the shape and condition of it and its relation to adjoining grants. Included also was the survey, which the applicant's friends usually made for him. It was made on horseback, with a measuring cord of braided rawhide. The petition assured the governor the applicant was a Mexican citizen, member of the church and married in it. In the right-hand margin space was left for the governor's reply.

"2. Typical questions the governor posed: Could the land be granted without injury to other parties? Was the applicant telling the truth about himself? This was addressed, not to the applicant, but to the prefect of the district.

"3. The prefect's reply (*informe*), attached to the petition, went back to the governor who, having satisfied himself all was well, issued the grant in form. The party then was accorded 'juridical possession' by officials on the scene."

According to Jack Tracy, "It took three years for Richardson to acquire *political possession* of his lands. In 1841, accompanied by his wife and children, the *Alcalde* from Sonoma, and two witnesses,

Richardson traveled on horseback, pausing at each *majonera* or landmark, where Richardson recited the required oath before witnesses. At the conclusion of the three-day journey, the *Alcalde* signed the papers stating that the petition complied with 'all formalities of the Law' (and there were many)." Perhaps, as was customary, Richardson took symbolic possession by pulling up clumps of grass, breaking the branches of trees or bushes, and throwing rocks in the four cardinal directions, thus indicating that as owner he could do things to the land that would not be permitted to another. In any event, "on October 15, 1841, the land became the undisputed property of Don Guillermo Antonio Richardson, to 'enjoy freely and exclusively, appropriating it to the culture and use that best suit him.'"

Now a landowner, Richardson imported cattle to run wild on his rancho, to mingle with the elk, deer, bear, bobcat, and mountain lion.

But, not content to be merely a passive ranchero, he invested heavily in maritime craft: several bay schooners, and three deep-water vessels—all of which, within a short space of time, went down in storms. Richardson suddenly found himself without cash. He mortgaged Rancho Saucelito for $60,000, at 3 percent a month, compounded monthly. In no time, he was unable to make the payments. Reserving 640 acres, which he had promised for his family, he deeded the ranch to one Samuel Throckmorton, who broke up the land into a group of dairy farms.

For years there were rumors and legends of buried gold on Rancho Saucelito. A forty-niner who had struck it rich, defecting secretly from a partner, would sneak into the headlands after dark, inter his treasure—and perhaps never return. True or false, gold or no gold, in 1856, Don Guillermo Antonio Richardson, a *persona de razon*, erstwhile owner of the ranch, died — penniless and in debt.

Richardson's survivors received the promised 640 acres. And that same day they turned around and sold it, for $7,500, to a group of investors — one of whom was Samuel Throckmorton. Soon thereafter, the group sold 1,200 acres, which included the 640, for $440,000.

Within ten years after Richardson's death, Throckmorton had realized over a million dollars — and still had most of the acreage left.

Before he died, Richardson had offered to sell the Lime Point Tract, the Golden Gate Headlands, to the U.S. government, as a military preserve. But his asking price — $400,000 — was too steep. Now Throckmorton, seeking further profits, entered into protracted negotiations. It was not until after the Civil War — in 1866 — that the tract, 1,889 acres, was finally acquired by the military, at a cost of $125,000.

Here, at the Golden Gate Headlands, a modern military presence was initiated.

◆　◆　◆

Battery Townsley

Nº 55-B
Battery Townsley
Fort Cronkhite, Calif.
Hill 417 ~ Loading Blast
Feb. 16, 1938

Nº 56-B
Battery Townsley
Fort Cronkhite, Calif.
Hill 417 ~ Blast
Feb. 16, 1938

20

Nº 39-B
Battery Townsley
Fort Cronkhite, Calif.
Drilling at Reservoir Site
Feb. 2, 1938

Fort Cronkhite, Calif.
Slide on Roadway to Hill 417
Sta. 93+75
Feb. 15, 1938

Nº 75 B
Fort Cronkhite, Calif.
Blast at Site for Gun Block Nº 2
March 25, 1940

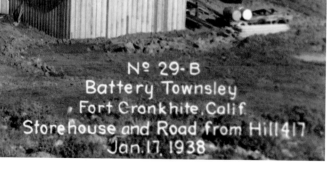

No 29-B
Battery Townsley
Fort Cronkhite, Calif.
Storehouse and Road from Hill 417
Jan. 17, 1938

23

24

No 243 B
Battery Townsley
Fort Cronkhite Calif.
Forms for A A Battery
Magazine, Power & Store Room
July 28, 1939

No. 249-B
Fort Cronkhite Calif.
A.A. Battery
Magazine & Power Room
Aug. 17 1939

26

No. 199-B
Battery Townsley
Fort Cronkhite, Calif.
Casemate No. 1
Applying Waterproofing
Oct. 14, 1938

No. 231-B
Battery Townsley
Fort Cronkhite, Calif.
Placing Racer Section
Carriage 15.
June 30, 1939

28

No. 157-B
Battery Townsley
Fort Cronkhite, Calif.
Casemate No. 1
Covering Waterproofed Roof
With Layer of Gravel For
Drainage.
Nov. 15, 1938

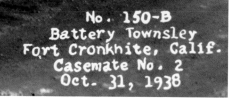

No. 150-B
Battery Townsley
Fort Cronkhite, Calif.
Casemate No. 2
Oct. 31, 1938

30

No. 238 B
Battery Townsley
Fort Cronkhite Calif.
Moving Gun No. 88 to
Gun Block No. 1
July 27 1939

No. 241 E
Battery Townsley
Fort Cronkhite Calif.
Placing Gun No 00 in Cradle
JULY 28 1939

● Vacant gun mount, Battery Smith Guthrie.

IN 1792, George Vancouver, spying on the Spanish settlement, reported that defenses consisted of "two useless guns."

Two years later, the Spaniards built *El Castillo de San Joaquin* on what was then called *Punta de Cantil Blanco*, now Fort Point, at the south end of Golden Gate. Six bronze and up to ten iron guns were mounted. These had been cast in Lima, Peru, and were already over a hundred years old before being brought to Alta California.

A year later — 1795 — a fort was proposed for Punta de San Carlos, or, as it was later called, Lime Point, at the north end of the gate. This was the first mention of fortifying the headlands. But nothing came of it.

When the United States seized California from Mexico, and the area was later (1850) admitted to statehood, "other nations watched with keen interest as the United States attempted to hold the vast new territory with a thin thread of military presence. . . ."

The army entered into negotiations for the Lime Point Tract, first with Richardson, later with Throckmorton — negotiations that dragged on through the years.

In 1858, although the government owned no land in the area, "a board of engineers recommended the construction of a large masonry fortification at Lime Point that would contain 250 guns (8- and 10-inch columbiads and 42-pounder smoothbores). But, as with earlier plans, this one languished.

During the Civil War the C.S.S. *Shenandoah* and other Confederate raiders attacked the Union commercial whaling fleet in North Pacific waters. One such raider threatened San Francisco, but the commanding officer was no doubt familiar with the guns at Fort Point, such as they were. He chose to remain outside the Farallons.

" . . . Attacks during the Civil War on various seacoast defense forts such as Fort Pulaski, Georgia, and the Union attack on Confederate-occupied Fort Sumter in 1864 demonstrated the obsolescence of such forts in the face of rifled artillery, whose shells, unlike the cannonballs fired from old smoothbore cannon, could breach their walls with ease. Fort Point was similar in design and construction to Fort Sumter. . . . "

"Rifling made artillery pieces both more powerful and more accurate than the previous smoothbore cannon. To counter the penetrating power of rifled artillery, a new system of defensive fortifications was required, employing either armor plating or thick earthen ramparts."

On July 24, 1866, the purchase of the Lime Point Tract from Samuel Throckmorton—1,889 acres of the Marin Headlands—was completed.

At once Col. George H. Mendell made plans for blasting the projecting cliff at Lime Point, in order to produce a platform at near water level on which a brick and masonry fort might be built similar to the one opposite at Fort Point.

"Mendell undertook experiments at Lime Point with nitroglycerine as a blasting agent. His first attempt to use it was a failure when the liquid ran off through seams in the rock. Succeeding trials were more successful, and later he obtained a new form of the explosive that had been mixed with sawdust. He informed the Engineer Department that this explosive agent was called 'dynamite' or 'giant powder.' In the end Mendell chose ordinary gunpowder as his blasting agent because its explosion threw a given mass in a specific direction. . . . "

"The engineers . . . excavated three tunnels deep into the cliff, each with a series of chambers which were packed with several thousand pounds of powder. By this process it was hoped that the whole face of the cliff could be blasted off down to the desired level.

"The first tunnel was begun on March 7, 1868 and completed on May 11. It was 125 feet in length and had two powder chambers six feet high and four feet wide packed with black powder. . . . These charges were exploded in April 1869.

"General B. S. Alexander of the Corps of Engineers was on hand to witness one of the explosions. He described it:

Everything being in readiness, the wires were connected with the little box, the machine set in motion, and the connections made, when lo! the mountain was seen in labor. There was no explosion in the popular sense of the term. A little smoke and flame was seen to escape through the moving mass of rock, and the whole face of the hill in front of the charges was seen to move outward, falling down into the sea. And then was seen a sight rarely witnessed, a hill without foundation giving away and tumbling into the depths below.

There was no noise from the powder, and not a stone was thrown fifty feet from its position by the force of the explosion. Yet the sight was grand, and being unaccompanied by any visible cause, was awful from its very silence. For about half a minute of time the masses of rock above came rolling down the face of the hill."

But nothing further happened. No fort was built. The concept of water-level batteries was already under scrutiny, this being the first episode in the long history of the coast artillery wherein the fortifications or guns, and their value, were questioned, often before they were completed or emplaced.

At Lime Point, in 1876, instead of building a fort, it was decided to survey the entire tract, the southern coast of the headlands, for possible battery sites. Lt.

Thomas H. Handbury received the task. "His first choice was the valley west of Lime Point, which he proposed naming Gravelly Beach. This valley contained about 25 acres and was large enough for six 'of our largest guns.'

"Point Diablo, Handbury found, was too small for a battery of modern guns. It could perhaps be cut down to about half its height (200 feet), and a monitor turret or something similar could be placed there. East of Point Bonita, the lieutenant noted a beach at which heavy guns could be planted. They would then have to be hauled up a 60-foot bluff. . . . "

"Handbury considered Point Bonita a suitable location for 'many' batteries of long-range guns. 'Among the old native residents and shippers of that vicinity,' he said, 'it is known by the name of North Point. It is a long narrow ridge jutting far out from the mainland and terminating in an L-shaped mass of rocks.' There was sufficient space for a snug little post: 'The northwest portion of the ground is a very good location for quarters, barracks and storehouses. It is sheltered from the winds and entirely out of the view of an enemy. In this vicinity, or in a little valley just north of it, ground may be found which will answer very well for drill purposes.' While the water of Rodeo Lagoon was brackish, Handbury located two or three 'never-failing springs of excellent water.' Concerning the beach at Rodeo Lagoon, he thought it possible that an enemy could land on it in calm weather. However, 'a short range gun, or two, placed upon either of the adjacent slopes would be sufficient' defense."

Barbette batteries were planned at Lime Point, including what came to be called Ridge Battery, "at an elevation of well over 400 feet on top of Lime Point Bluff." Construction was completed in 1879, and it was intended as the site for four fifteen-inch Rodman cannons and four mortars.

One writer claims that with all the plans for gun emplacements in this period, only two were ever built. " . . . And in 1873 a single gun, a fifteen-inch smoothbore Rodman, was installed. For the next fifteen years, that gun and the rusty old fog signal at Point Bonita were the only protection for the north shore of Golden Gate."

The battery at Gravelly Beach was completed in 1870, about the same time as Ridge Battery. It was intended to hold twelve Rodman cannons, but only one was mounted.

Earthen fortifications at Lime Point, in the 1870s and 1880s, were tunneled by gophers. The pilings of the wharf were eaten out by the *teredo*, or ship worm.

In 1893 the forward positions of Cliff Battery were purposely destroyed, to make room for what would later become Battery Spenser.

"During the 1870s and 1880s American industry developed the capability of forging and tooling large steel components such as gun tubes of great size and length. New tooling capabilities made possible heavy, tightly machined, complex steel breech mechanisms. New explosives such as grained powder were created whose rate of burning could be controlled by regulating grain size and other factors. Instead of the single sharp kick given by a gunpowder explosion, the new explosives could be tailor-made to burn more slowly, at varying rates, to suit the lengths of particular gun tubes, giving a sustained and increasing push to the shell for the full length of its journey through a much longer tube, thus greatly increasing range and accuracy of fire. Simultaneously, the invention of new types of pillar, pedestal, barbette and retracting gun carriages, the most complex perhaps being the Buffington-Crozier so-called 'disappearing' carriage which used the recoil force of firing to retract the gun rearward and downward to a point where it could be reloaded behind the protection from enemy fire provided by massive breastworks, called for new design of gun emplacements."

During the 1890s the building of new batteries proceeded slowly. But, as was the case in every war, "the pace quickened dramatically with the outbreak of the Spanish-American War. . . . "

By then "the concept of sea-power had taken such a hold on the American public that a real fear of foreign naval attacks had developed."

"For a unique combination of geographical, historical reasons, seacoast fortification represented a peculiarly attractive means of defense in the United States, where at times it was carried on to an extent paralleled by few other nations. Here, as a recent military historian has observed, the emphasis on this particular form of protection 'was to grow virtually into an obsession' and lead toward the end of the nineteenth century to a program of harbor defense that became almost a substitute for any other form of military policy."

"This concern with fortification of seaports, which persisted as late as World

No. 226-B
Gun No. 88 in Transit from
Waldo, Calif.
June 26, 1939

War II, stemmed to some extent from the genuine defensive requirements imposed by this country's geography. Throughout its history, the powers that represented the most serious and most likely threats to its security lay across the seas rather than within this hemisphere. In addition, the Unites States, because of its extended coastlines and numerous coastal cities, simply had more points requiring such defense than did most other nations. These facts, however, cannot alone account for the American preoccupation with seacoast fortification, which must to a large degree be attributed to several long-enduring and interrelated attitudes and traditions, some dating back to our early colonial history. Most of these, basically unaltered with time except in terms of their specific end-products, still survive to affect today the steps being taken for national defense, much as they did a hundred years ago.

"One such attitude is that of the militia concept and the related attitude of opposition to military professionalism and a large regular army. This concept was linked with defense against sea-borne attack from the earliest colonial days, when the lack of military forces and the absence of reliable interior communications made it necessary for each settlement to prepare a battery of at least two or three guns that could be manned by the local populace in the event of danger form the sea. . . .

"Of such defenses, wrote Henry W. Halleck in 1843:

When once constructed they require but little expenditure for their support. In time of peace they withdraw no valuable citizens from their useful occupations of life. Of themselves they can never exert an influence dangerous to public liberty; but as the means of preserving peace, and as obstacles to an invader, their influence and power are immense.

"Halleck's phrase, . . . as the means of preserving peace, reflects still another attitude common among Americans — that security can be purchased, and mass mobilization avoided, perhaps entirely — by enough of the right kinds of military hardware. As war has grown in technical complexity, so has this attitude, and the obvious parallels between seacoast fortifications . . . and many of the post-World War II 'weapons systems,' in terms of the security promised by both, need hardly be pointed out."

President Grover Cleveland, December 1896: "We should always keep in mind that of all forms of military preparation coast defense alone is essentially pacific in nature. While it gives the sense of security due to a consciousness of strength, it is neither the purpose nor the effect of such permanent fortifications to involve us in foreign complications, but rather to guarantee us against them. They are not temptation to war, but security against it. Thus, they are thoroughly in accord with all the traditions of our national diplomacy."

Battery Spencer:

"Three 12-inch BL rifles (model 1888m nos. 10, 16, and 17) came from the Watervliet Arsenal, mounted on non-disappearing carriages (model 1892, nos. 1, 4, and 5), Watertown Arsenal. This battery was named in GO 16, February 14, 1902, in honor of Maj. Gen. Joseph Spencer, Continental Army, 1775 – 1778, who died in 1789."

Battery Kirby:

"Two 12-inch RL rifles (model 1895, nos. 12 and 16) came from the Watervliet Arsenal, mounted on disappearing carriages (model 1897, nos. 14 and 15) and manufactured by the Morgan Engineering Company. This battery was named in GO 16, February 14, 1902, in honor of Lt. Edmund Kirby, who died on May 28, 1863, from wounds received on May 3 at the Battle of Chancellorsville, Virginia. Kirby was promoted to brigadier general of volunteers on the day he died."

Battery Mendell:

"Two 12-inch BL rifles (model 1895, nos. 4B and 6), Bethlehem Steel Company; mounted on disappearing carriages (model 1897, nos. 30 and 31) that were manufactured by Midvale Steel Company. This first battery at Point Bonita was named in GO 120, dated November 22, 1902, in honor of Col. George H. Mendell, Corps of Engineers, who had more to do with the defenses of San Francisco than any other engineer officer. He died in San Francisco in 1902."

Battery Alexander:

"Eight 12-inch BL mortars (model 1890, nos. 145, 147, 148, 150, 151, 155, 159, 160) came from the Watervliet Arsenal mounted on carriages, model 1896 (converted into model 1896 MI) nos. 277, 278, 279, 280, 281, 282, 283, and 284, made by Rarig Engineering Company. This mortar battery was named in GO 120, November 22, 1902, in honor of Col. Barton S. Alexander, Corps of Engineers. Alexander served with distinction in both the Mexican and Civil Wars. At the time of his death, 1878, he was senior engineer on the Pacific Coast and the friend and associate of Colonel Mendell above."

Barry, Fort, Calif.

"Permanent post, located at entrance to San Francisco Bay, adjoining Fort Baker, Marin County. Named in honor of Col. William F. Barry, 2nd Arty., U.S.A. (Bvt. Maj. Gen.), who served as Chief of Arty., Army of the Potomac, during the Peninsula Campaign, 1862. Established as separate reservation, 1904, from lands originally part of Fort Baker. Station of Coast Defenses of San Francisco (North Pacific Coast Artillery District). Area — About 1,344 acres."

Battery Guthrie:

"Originally four 6-inch rapid-fire guns (model 1900, nos. 2, 3, 5, and 12) came from Watervliet Arsenal,

● Gun No. 88 in transit from Waldo, California, June 26, 1939.

mounted on barbette carriages (model 1900, nos. 13, 14, 15, and 16) made at the Rock Island Arsenal. These emplacements were named in GO 194, December 27, 1904, in honor of Capt. Edwin Guthrie, 15th Infantry, who died of wounds received in action at La Hoya, Mexico, in 1847."

Battery Rathbone:

"Originally four 6-inch rapid-fire guns (model 1900, nos. 19, 29, 33, and 34) manufactured at the Watervliet Arsenal. They were mounted on barbette carriages (model 1900, nos. 42, 43, 44) from the Builder's Iron Foundry and No. 26 from the Watervliet Arsenal. This battery was named in GO 194, December 27, 1904, in honor of Lt. Samuel B. Rathbone, U. S. Artillerists, who died of wounds received in the attack on Queenstown Heights, Upper Canada, in 1812."

Battery O'Rorke:

"Four 15-pounder, 3-inch guns on pedestal mounts, barbette carriages (model 1903, nos. 68, 69, 70, 71) came from Watertown Arsenal. . . . This battery was named in GO 194, December 27, 1904, in honor of Col. Patrick Henry O'Rorke, born in Ireland and a West Point graduate, who was killed at the Battle of Gettysburg, Pennsylvania, in July 1863."

All the batteries were constructed, now, of concrete, which was cheap and durable. But as rapidly as they were finished and operational, deficiencies were demonstrated. Battery Spenser, completed in 1897, was the subject of a 1904 report: "Shot rooms had insufficient capacity. Powder magazines had insufficient capacity. There was only one powder magazine for guns 1 and 2. Galleries were too narrow. Galleries were too crooked. No storage space was available for armament chests, sponges, etc. Only one ammunition hoist was needed per gun. There was no means of returning empty shot trucks to magazine with sufficient rapidity. There were no latrines. There was no commanding officer's room. There was no guardroom. There

GENERAL ORDERS NO. 43

WAR DEPARTMENT, WASHINGTON, March 30, 1908

The following is published to the Army for the information and guidance of all concerned:

The military reservations of Forts Baker and Barry together form a tract of land having an area of 1,899.66 acres, situated and embracing the north side of the 'Golden Gate' or entrance to the harbor of San Francisco, in Marin County, California. A true north and south line through 'Point Diablo' separated the tract into two reservations — the eastern portion retaining the name of Fort Baker, and the western portion (known as 'Point Bonita') having been named Fort Barry by General Orders, No. 194, War Department, December 27, 1904. The metes and bounds of the said tract, according to the deed to the United States from Samuel R. Throckmorton, dated July 24, 1866 (recorded in Liber F, pages 127–30 of the deed records of Marin County), and the plat of survey attached to and made a part of said deed, certified September 29, 1860, by W. J. Lewis, United States deputy Surveyor, are as follows:

Beginning at a point on the most eastern rock seen above water of a ledge of rocks extending into the Bay of San Francisco, from the wooded hill connecting with the high spur which limits the Cove of Sausalito to the south, and which point is designated by a copper bolt marked 'O' being the initial point of the survey . . . " etc., etc.

"BY ORDER OF THE SECRETARY OF WAR:
J. FRANKLIN BELL,
Major General, Chief of Staff.

OFFICIAL:

HENRY F. McCAIN,
Adjutant General.

● Twelve-inch seacoast rifle firing at night, possibly Battery Wallace, n.d., circa 1930.

was no place to install other booths where they would be protected in action. There was no communication by speaking tube, or other means, between guns, magazines, etc. Battery parade should be on level with magazine floors to enable ammunition to be hoisted from the parade in an emergency. There should be an entrance to the galleries from each gun to afford more light and freer access to the parade. Ammunition hoists were mechanically unsatisfactory. There was no permanent lookout for battery commander (BC station). There was no storage space for waste, cleaning materials, spare emergency parts, and policing tools and implements. There were no conduits for telephone and other wires. There were too few magazines to allow proper segregation of loaded shells."

The newer batteries incorporated improvements, and also accommodated the greater size and range of the newer guns. Beginning at Lime Point, where the first guns had a range of perhaps two miles, the batteries migrated northwestward, to Point Bonita and beyond, affording protection to an ever-widening range of the approach to Golden Gate.

"Just as the Civil War had shown the masonry forts to be obsolete, the modern guns of Germany in 1914 demonstrated that the Belgium fortifications of the 1890s were out of date. Also alarming the American officers was the British production of the *Queen Elizabeth* class of battleships in 1914, with its 15-inch guns. The chief of engineers informed the chief of staff that America's coastal guns must be at least as great a caliber and must have at least as great a range as the naval guns. He recommended that Congress au-

thorize a certain number of new seacoast emplacements each year just as it then authorized a certain number of new warships annually. The major caliber direct-fire gun, he said, should be the immense 16-inch rifle. And he recommended an annual appropriation of $5,500,000 for fortification construction.

"While the 16-inch gun might be the major direct-fire weapon of the future, that did not mean that the 12-inch rifles were obsolete. The War Department noted that by changing the carriage of the 12-inch gun so as to increase its elevation to a minimum of 15 degrees and by decreasing the weight of the projectile, to about 800 pounds, an effective range of 22,000 yards could be achieved. This range would make the 12-inch guns practically equal to that of any guns that might be brought against them."

Earlier, in 1911, two events occurred that, although no one knew it at the time, foreshadowed the end of all coastal artillery:

One: "In January 1911, an air show was held at San Francisco. On the 15th of that month Lieutenant Myron C. Crissy, riding in a Wright biplane with Philip Parmalee as pilot, released manually a 61-pound bomb upon a target. He was the first United States officer to drop an explosive missile from an airplane."

Two: "During the air show some imaginative naval officers had constructed a wooden platform on the cruiser Pennsylvania which was anchored in the bay. On January 18, pilot Eugene Ely landed a Curtis pusher on this platform and then successfully took off again."

"By 1915 the nations of Europe had

gone to war, and the United States was maintaining a wary neutrality. In 1914 the San Francisco engineer prepared plans and estimates for a new rapid-fire 5-inch battery at Fort Miley — but not because of the war in Europe, rather because of a crisis involving relations with Japan.

"Anti-Japanese sentiment had long been an important force in the politics of California, particularly in San Francisco. In 1913 the California legislature, with the support of Governor Hiram Johnson, passed the Alien Land Law. This law limited the Japanese from leasing or purchasing agricultural land within the state. The Japanese government protested vigorously. And the United States Army took emergency measures to strengthen its Pacific defenses. From May to September, a steady stream of personnel, weapons, ammunition, and supplies moved through the Army's port at Fort Mason."

Fear of attack by sea . . . and fear now, for the first time, of attack by air:

In 1916, just five years after the exploits at the Air Show, "The district engineer Thomas Rees prepared plans and estimates for antiaircraft guns for the defense of San Francisco. . . . His project called for six 3-inch antiaircraft guns. . . . Each concrete circle was to be 30 feet in diameter so as to facilitate sponging the guns. The floors of the rooms between the emplacements were to be three feet lower than the gun platforms."

In 1917 the United States entered the Great War, and construction began on the newest of the batteries at Fort Barry, Battery Wallace, named in honor of Col. Elmer J. Wallace who had died just recently of wounds received in France.

"Two 12-inch guns were mounted on

barbette carriages. . . . Battery Wallace differed from the earlier 12-inch batteries in that modifications were made to its carriages that allowed for a greater angle of elevation. This factor plus a lighter projectile increased the range of the guns by almost 12,000 feet."

It had long been noted that "visibility conditions in San Francisco Bay presented great difficulties. Dense fog was prevalent for a large part of the year and heavy haze was not unusual. High fogs, 100 feet or higher above the water, were common. On occasions it was possible to see a target clearly from the north shore, while fog hid it from southern shore stations. 'Bearing these conditions in mind,' one report stated, 'it is desirable to supply a right and left handed baseline for all major armament, and for the extremely long range armament, supplementary flank stations in addition to the normal baselines. For the same reasons all batteries should be supplied with at least one low station each.'

"Long-range-armament, such as Battery Wallace, required a minimum of five observation stations located between San Pedro Point to the south and Gull Rock to the north. Other primary armament, such as Battery Mendell, needed four stations so as to provide northern and southern baselines and a low-fog station fairly close to the battery."

Access to Fort Barry had long been a problem, because of the steep hills. With the advent of the war — and particularly, with the increasing size and weight of the guns to be moved—the problems became urgent, and it was decided to construct a tunnel.

"During the war years construction work was pushed and the tunnel was finally completed in 1918. It was the most ambitious piece of engineering accomplished on the northern headlands since Mendell's blasting operations at Lime Point Bluff. The tunnel was cut almost entirely through rock, although some of it was so soft that it crumbled. Consequently, it was necessary to line it with timber. Dimensions of the tunnel were sixteen feet wide and sixteen feet high. The lining consisted of ten-inch x ten-inch timber sets placed on an average of five feet apart and covered on the outside by two-inch lagging. When completed, the tunnel was approximately 2,200 feet long."

In 1935 the tunnel was enlarged and improved, and the state of California added 100 feet in 1954.

Another construction project — this one in 1921—was the balloon hanger, built to house the balloons that were used for observation purposes in the firing of the larger coastal guns. The hanger stands today, "a large structure and of awkward design." It is one of only two on the West Coast.

Battery Hamilton A. Smith

"In 1922, Battery Edwin Guthrie was divided for better management of the weapons, the two guns on the left flank becoming Battery Hamilton A. Smith in accordance with GO 13 dated March 22, 1922. Smith was a West Point graduate who was killed in action at Soissons, France, in 1918. He was awarded the Distinguished Service Cross posthumously.

During World War I the power of enemy air attack had been demonstrated, and this was further evident from the

work of General Billy Mitchell in the 1920s. Accordingly, the batteries housing the bigger guns were given greater earthen and concrete protection, and the first camouflage nets came into use. At the same time, the guns grew ever larger, with greater range and accuracy. As early as 1915, the installation of the mighty 16-inch guns on the Marin Headlands had become "a matter of serious discussion." "These guns had a range of roughly 26 miles, a far cry from the two and a half mile range of the guns of the 1850s, which could barely control the narrowest part of Golden Gate Strait between Fort Point and Lime Point. These larger modern guns could instead keep an enemy fleet far out to sea, hopefully far enough so that enemy guns would not be in range of the city and harbor."

"But the guns were not built for many years. It was not until the 1937 appropriation that Congress approved expenditure of funds for the purchase of land at Tennessee Point on which to build the immense battery." [The army already owned the coastal area of Tennessee Point as part of a searchlight project. Powerful searchlights were mounted along the coast of San Francisco Bay to illuminate any sort of nocturnal enemy invasion or attack.] "The army acquired about 800 acres north of Rodeo Lagoon and northwest of Fort Barry by condemnation in 1937, the deed being recorded on June 21."

"In General Orders 9, December 17, 1937, the army named this new reservation *Fort Cronkhite* in honor of Maj. Gen. Adelbert Cronkhite, an old artilleryman who had recently died."

"In March 1938 excavation on Wolf Ridge for the new firing platforms began. In a secret letter dated December 31, 1937, the new battery was named for General Clarence P. Townsley, who had commanded the 30th Infantry Division in France in World War I and who had died in 1928."

"As early as 1929 estimates had been prepared for 16-inch guns on Wolf Ridge, and in 1935 the district engineer at San Francisco, Lt. Col. H. A. Finch, had begun working on plans for a battery of 16-inch guns there, for the day when it would become a military reservation. By the end of 1937, these plans had been revised several times and brought to completion. . . . Here at Cronkhite the gun casemates and the firing platforms would be built as one continuous operation. The two would not be monolithic in nature because, said the engineers, gun-firing impacts were instantaneous, whereas machinery vibrations were continuous. Furthermore, the engineers wanted to 'shock-insulate' the casemate-firing platform combinations from the remainder of the magazine structure by an inset of 4 inches of creosoted lumber in key between the casemates and the magazine. Another modification called for placing the radio station in the same structure as the plotting/switchboard rooms rather than in a building by itself. . . . Also, . . . the engineers no longer wanted a sunken gallery at the entrance of the plotting/switchboard rooms. Such a gallery served to trap gas around the air lock door."

"While a geological report stated that tunneling would be feasible providing it

were done in the summer, the engineers decided it would be costly and hazardous. When in March 1938 excavation of the firing platforms began, the engineers found that most of the rock was badly shattered chert; this convinced them that cut-and-cover was desirable for the magazine traverse. The excavated material, although rock, was approved for backfill, there being no problem concerning flying rock at a casemated work."

"Mindful of complaints . . . , the engineers had this battery's latrines incorporated with the main work."

"Because of its isolated location, Battery Townsley got its own reserve magazine. This large five-room structure was located behind a hill some 700 yards to the east."

"Battery Townsley and its reserve magazine both were completed and transferred to the Coast Artillery Corps in July 1940. On July 1, the first 16-inch round ever fired from the Pacific Coast of the continental United States was fired here.
"In addition to Battery Townsley, an antiaircraft battery designated AA Battery No. 1 consisting of three 3-inch guns was completed on Wolf Ridge above Battery Townsley on August 26, 1940. In July 1941, three batteries of mobile 155 mm. guns were similarly emplaced, and over a period of years five fire control stations were built on Wolf Ridge."

"At the time Battery Townsley was constructed it was the most modern of seacoast defense sites in the San Francisco Bay area. . . . It had an overhead projection similar to the later casemate at Battery

Wallace to protect the gun from aerial bombardment as well as high angle naval weapons. It was armed with two 16-inch long range rifles, the largest in the Headlands, with ranges of 45,100 yards and was used for testing more than any of the other weapons because of its isolated coastal position."

December 7, 1941 — Pearl Harbor Day — found Forts Barry and Cronkhite, like most of the rest of the country, less than fully prepared — at least in the military mind. Barracks and other buildings at Cronkhite were rushing to completion, antiaircraft protection was inadequate, and the process of mining the harbor was incomplete.
The placing of harbor mines had a long history. "Torpedoes, later called mines, were an American invention. An unsuccessful attempt was made to destroy a British warship with one as early as the Revolutionary War. Robert Fulton blew up a small vessel with one early in the 19th century."

"Electrically fired 'torpedoes' or mines required a control room from which cables ran out into the water and from which an operator sent the electrical impulse to fire the mine. . . . "

"Fields of both shore-controlled mines and some contact mines were planted near San Francisco during the late 1930s and early 1940s. . . . "

"The submarine mine project was only partially installed on December 7, 1941. Exhaustive efforts were made to place additional groups of mines during the first months of the war. Extremely bad

● Cutting up the big guns for scrap metal, n.d., circa 1948.

weather in December and January hampered the work. On the night of December 14, mine vessel L-74 was grounded and sunk by heavy seas; yet, the mines were laid and the channels defended."

"In June 1942 a navy blimp reported that an enemy mine-laying submarine was operating at the west end of Main Channel outside the American minefield. The blimp did not see the submarine itself; it 'saw' many submerged mines in the area. The army closed Main Channel for five hours while the navy conducted sweeping operations in the area. The report remained silent on the results of the sweep."

Immediately after Pearl Harbor, Battery Townsley went on fifteen-minute alert . . . the guns to be ready for firing on that much notice. "For at least a year after Pearl Harbor, 150 men lived *within* the battery."

After the war, the following account came to light — written by the commander of "I-15," a Japanese submarine operating just off the coast.

"On December 17, 1941, through my binoculars I could see glow cast upon the sky by the lights of San Francisco, and thought to myself, 'They certainly don't act like there is a war going on, allowing such illumination to silhouette their shipping along the coast.'

"A few days after we got on station, I-15 and other submarines received a wireless from Vice Adm. Shimuzu. We were to depart our control areas on Christmas Day and return to Kwajalein, where he had his headquarters. But first he had

a special present he wanted delivered to America — all the rounds of 4.7-inch ammunition we could pour out of our deck guns. All nine submarines were to shell the mainland, I-15's target being San Francisco. On Dec. 24, just hours before I-15 was to commence its bombardment, this order was countermanded by one from Tokyo, sent by Adm. Osami Nagano. I never learned the reason why."

In 1942 construction began on the last and perhaps most elaborate gun emplacement on the headlands: *Battery Construction 129.* It remained known by this informal name, since no battery was formally named until fully operational, which never happened at 129. The battery was designed to house two massive 16-inch guns, weighing one million pounds each, capable of firing 2,100-pound shells a distance of twenty-seven miles, with accuracy.

Hill 129, above Point Diablo, is the highest point on the headlands, 800 feet above sea level. Approximately a million cubic yards of concrete were poured. Walls and floors were eight to twelve feet thick. To produce the concrete a gravel quarry was opened in the headlands. The crushed rock was transported up the hill, to be mixed and poured. In the concrete ceilings of the tunnels a monorail system was mounted, to move the shells.

By 1943 construction was nearly 100 percent complete — battery commander's station, plotting/switchboard/radio rooms, etc. But bringing in the guns from Sausalito presented a problem. Back in the 1940s there were few cranes or similar devices available to lift such immense weight. It was decided to place each gun on a trailer pulled by several trucks, each

traveling at precisely the same speed and engine RPM in order to get the maximum power.

There is a story — apocryphal — that one of the guns, being dragged through the tunnel, became stuck. The solution? "'The war just about had to stop,' recalled one citizen soldier, 'while we considered that situation. But did we fail? No, siree. It took fifty tons of Vaseline, but we got the gun through.'"

By whatever method, the guns arrived at the site.

But they were never mounted. Even though, as at Battery Townsley, dummy roads were constructed to confuse an aerial attacker, it was decided, at the last minute, that since the war had shifted far to the west, installation of the guns would be postponed. In fact, they never were. Battery Construction 129 fell into a long tradition.

In 1948 the guns were declared surplus. "Toward the end of 1948, 'operation Blow-torch' got underway when the Richard Pierce Industrial Engineer Company of San Francisco began cutting the huge barrels into 5-foot sections, each weighing about 23 tons. The steel 'scrap' was sold to the Pacific States Steel company for resmelting." Some of the steel went to the Gillette Safety Razor Company, to make razor blades.

◆ ◆ ◆

● Battery Townsley, August 1939.

● Battery Townsley, October 1987.

● Fort Cronkhite, n.d., circa 1940.

● Fort Cronkhite: Park Visitors' Center, Headlands Institute, Pacific Energy Center, Headlands Center for the Arts studios, October 1987.

● Battery Townsley, Fort Cronkhite, B.C. Station prior to backfill, July 29, 1939.

● B.C. Station backfilled and overgrown, Hill 88, October 1987.

No. 249-B
Fort Cronkhite Calif.
A.A. Battery
Magazine & Power Room
Aug. 17, 1939

● Battery Townsley, Fort Cronkhite, AA battery, magazine and power room, August 1939.

● AA battery magazine in October 1987.

● Top of Hill 88, Wolf Ridge, n.d., circa 1939.

● Top of Hill 88, Wolf Ridge, October 1987.

433459

● Fort Barry, overview from upper Fort Cronkhite test area, December 22, 1953.

55

● Fort Barry from above old road on Wolf Ridge, January 1988.

56

● Painting in the "Temple of Love," former searchlight station.

DOWN through the years the followers of various trades and professions have placed themselves under the care and guidance of particular saints: patron saints.

For artillerists, the patron saint has long been St. Barbara — known, affectionately, as St. Babs.

In some ways she is a curious choice: "Usuardus and Ado in their martyrologies make St. Barbara a martyr in Tuscany; Metaphrastes says she suffered at Heliopolis; Baronius, in the Roman Martyrology, sets her down as martyr at Nicomedia. One authority is just as right as the other, for S. Barbara is a wholly mythical personage."

Her story, or legend, however, is colorful: "There was once upon a time a very wealthy and noble Greek named Dioscorus, an idolator, who had a daughter so beautiful in face and form that he shut her up in a tower, very lofty and inaccessible, so that no man might see her, and that thus she might be kept out of mischief. According to one account, however, he allowed her to take lessons of masters, of advanced age, or no doubt, of disagreeable appearance.

"At last Dioscorus determined to marry her to a suitable partner, but when he broached the subject, he found his daughter wholly opposed to the scheme. By some means or other the lovely Barbara had imbibed the doctrines of the gospel, and had resolved to dedicate her virginity to God. Her father was about to go on a long journey. Before he departed, she expressed to him her desire to have a bath constructed at the basement of her tower, in which she could disport herself, and while away the tediousness of the long hours of her incarceration. Dioscorus consented, but gave strict orders to the workmen to make two windows to this bath so high in the wall as to be inaccessible to any impudent and forward youth who might desire to look in whilst Barbara was splashing in her bath. The judicious father departed before the bath was completed. Barbara urged on the workmen the insufficiency of two windows, and insisted on their making a third. After great hesitation they consented to make a third opening. Barbara drew her finger on the marble rim of the bath, and a cross remained furrowed in the stone. On the return of Dioscorus from his journey, he was surprised and indignant at finding three windows to the bath-room instead of two. . . .

"Dioscorus was furious; he drew his sword and rushed upon the maiden to put her to death. But suddenly the rock cleft, received her into its bosom, and left Dioscorus striking furiously on its flinty surface.

"The excited and astonished parent tore about the mountain looking for his daughter. She had, in the meantime, slipped out of the rock at a distance from the tower. . . . The father found her, kicked and beat her, and drew her by the hair before the chief magistrate, Marcian. . . .

"Marcian . . . gave sentence that she . . . should be executed with the sword.

" . . . Barbara prayed. On reaching the

destined place, her father cut off her head. . . . A flash of lightening fell and consumed Dioscorus, another flash reduced Marcian to a smoking ashheap. Accordingly S. Barbara is held to be the patroness of firearms. . . ."

Perhaps, in her own way, St. Babs *has* been a blessing to the artillerists of the headlands. In all the years of designing and constructing the batteries, of importing and emplacing guns, of training and retraining the crews, of target practice and endless maintenance — never once has a gun been fired in anger.

In recent years devil worshipers have invaded some of the tunnels in the fortifications, holding ceremonies, complete with animal sacrifices.

There are graffiti to be found at Townsley, Construction 129, and elsewhere:

MEAT IS MURDER
BIG BAD BLUE BOMB BITCH
METAL ON METAL IS THE ONLY WAY
TO HELL WITH TOMARROW LET'S LIVE
FOR TODAY
I ALWAYS THERR WHEN YOU THINK
I'M NOT
THE BEST DRESSED SOLDIER CAN'T
BE SEEN
SAVATAGE
MEGADEATH
METALLICA
No Man is to
Great to look
The other way
Especially
At times of
Death
HAVE A GOOD TIME ALL OF THE TIME

Have UFOs been sighted in the headlands?

HAVE YOU CHECKED ALL OF THE SAFETY POINTS.
IS THERE A MAN STANDING BY THE ELEVATOR MAIN POWER SWITCH.
CHECK TO SEE THAT ALL PERSONNEL ARE CLEAR OF THE OPERATING AREA.
ARE ALL MISSILES CLEAR OF THE ELEVATOR OR MOUNTED PROPERLY ON THE ELEVATOR.
EXIT. EXIT. EXIT (everywhere — in case the fuel caught on fire).

These are signs to be seen in the underground storage areas of the Nike missile sites, Fort Cronkhite.

And above ground, on the barbed wire fence:

CAUTION: THIS AREA PATROLLED BY SENTRY DOGS.

"Development started in 1964 on a surface-to-air missile that came to be called the Nike-Ajax. These rocket missiles were controlled by a computer that was 'fed' by three radars. One radar tracked the target; one followed the missile itself; and the third 'acquisition' radar detected distant aircraft and transferred the information to the target-tracking radar. In the late 1960s, the Nike-Hercules began to replace Nike-Ajax. The new missile was larger, faster and had a much greater range."

At Fort Barry, "The missile site lies fenced and official-looking still on the west side of Field Road. Nicknamed Battery Bravo, it was

● Defense icon, entrance to abandoned Nike radar installation on Wolf Ridge.

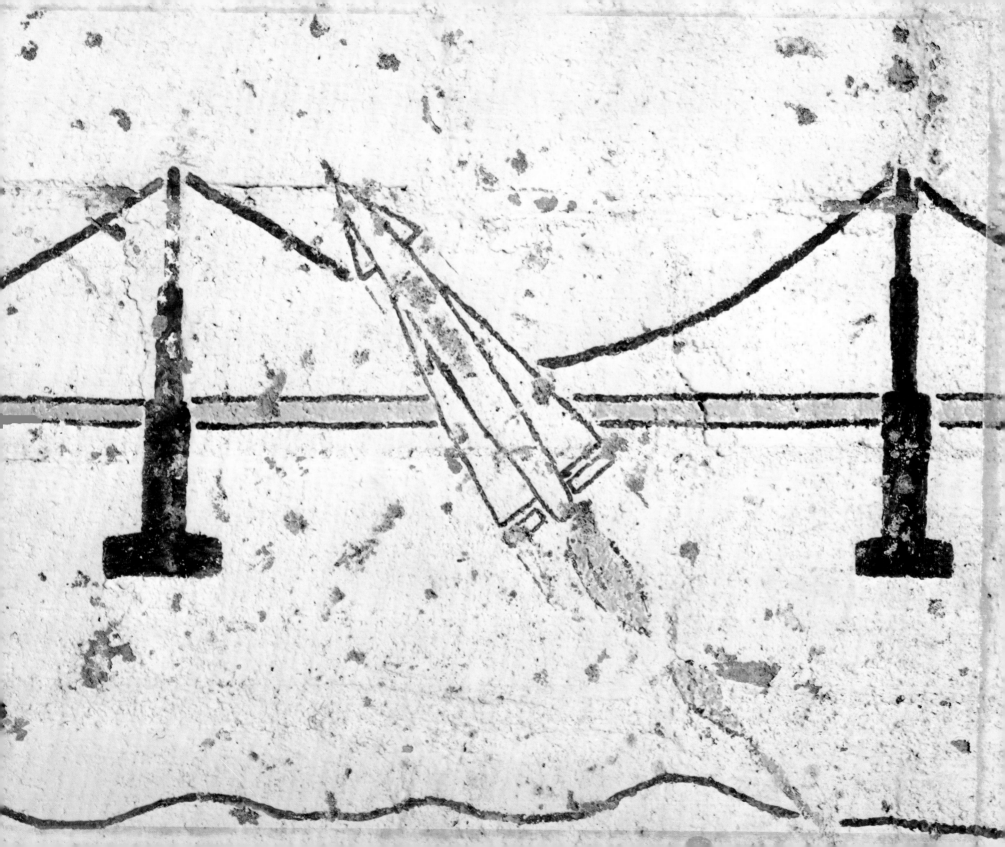

built in 1954 and deactivated in 1974, and in its time housed both the twenty-five-mile range Ajax missile and the eighty-seven-mile range Hercules, both of which could shoot horizontally or vertically after being raised on a huge elevator from their resting place under the earth. The radar station on Hill 88 in Fort Cronkhite directed the missile's course from their launching pad."

"Nike-Hercules is the first combat-ready surface-to-air missile with an atomic capability to enter active air defenses of the United States. It has been deployed with units of the United States Army Air Defense Command since June, 1958.

"It is the second 'generation' of the Army's Nike family of supersonic air defense missiles, and represents effectiveness many times over its predecessor, Nike-Ajax. What Nike-Ajax can do against single targets, Nike-Hercules can accomplish against entire formations of aircraft and do it with greater lethality. . . .

"Nike-Hercules has a range of more than 75 miles. In its secondary mission, as a surface-to-surface missile, it has been test fired at a range of 100 miles. Its altitude capability ranges from less than 1,000 feet to more than 150,000 feet (over 28 miles). Hercules is a direct outgrowth of the Nike-Ajax research and development program, and its universal-type ground control equipment permits both Nike-Hercules and Nike-Ajax to be fired from the same launcher area and to be directed by the same guidance equipment. In fact, the Hercules system actually improves the lethality of Ajax by acquiring and attacking targets at far greater ranges, higher altitudes, and greater speeds. The Nike-Hercules covers the range from very low altitudes to altitudes far in excess of any known drone-type or ram-jet missiles, or manned aircraft.

"With its booster, Nike-Hercules weighs approximately five tons and has an overall

length of 41 1/2 feet. The missile alone is 27 feet long and has a diameter of 32 inches. Its cluster of four boosters is 14 1/2 feet long. Nike-Hercules is a two-stage missile using a solid-fueled propellent rocket motor to sustain it in flight. Solid fuels are superior to liquid fuels in ease of handling, safety, and speed of preparing missiles for firing.

"Hercules has scored high-altitude kills against targets flying greater than 1,800 miles per hour (Mach 2.5). Full altitude capabilities of Nike-Hercules have never been tested because of lack of suitable targets."

"The guard dogs at this site were German Shepherds, a breed especially suited for this kind of work.

"During the daylight hours, the dogs were either in their kennels or undergoing training. At these times, both of the guard shacks on the site were manned. During the evening hours, only the shack at the main entrance was manned and the dogs patrolled between the two fenced areas."

"Guard dogs are almost always the traditional 'one man' dog and can only be approached by their trainer. If something should happen to the the trainer, guard dogs often cannot be retrained to another human and must be put away."

When a soldier-trainer was transferred, his dog probably went with him.

In the Bay Area, in the 1950s, a state of readiness rotated secretly from one Nike missile base to another.

The Nikes were characteristic of the period, of the Cold War. Secrecy was the key — and security was intense. "Most of the men who worked in one aspect of missile operations, such as guidance, radar, or maintenance, rarely got to know the people in other aspects of missile operations. This was primarily to keep

one person from knowing too much about how the Nike system operated." And if an authorized visitor went into the storage area, he was accompanied by an escort who stayed within eye or voice contact at all times.

Practically all the men working at the Nike sites had requested to be there. It was considered a desirable duty, despite the inherent dangers. These men were especially patriotic, conscious of defending "our homes" — defending America.

"The men who operate the Nike sites are something of a new breed of soldier. Many of the men don't live on post. They are members of the community they protect — buy homes there, send their children to local schools, lead Boy Scout Troops, and belong to civic clubs."

Unlike the fortifications, which were based on European models, the Nikes were an American invention—and were uniquely American.

United States Army Air Defense Command: "Whatever tomorrow may bring . . . NIKE will be watching, always ready."

"In the world today, a sincere desire for peace is not enough to guard us and our families. We must be ready to protect ourselves with the newest weapons science can provide. To man the equipment, the Army provides the best trained men available."

"In case of an enemy air attack on this country, those of us who live or work near our target areas might face great devastation. Safety could not be measured by the distance of a few dozen miles from the target."

"Should that day ever come—and only then —Nike will go into action to remove the enemy threat while it is still far distant in the sky and aid in preventing such devastation."

● Nike missile (inoperative), underground at Battery Bravo.

TREATY BETWEEN THE UNITED STATES OF AMERICA AND THE UNION OF SOVIET SOCIALIST REPUBLICS ON THE LIMITATION OF ANTI-BALLISTIC MISSILE SYSTEMS

The United States of America and the Union of Soviet Socialist Republics, hereinafter referred to as the Parties,

Proceeding from the premise that nuclear war would have devastating consequences for all mankind,

Considering that effective measures to limit anti-ballistic missile systems would be a substantial factor in curbing the race in strategic offensive arms and would lead to a decrease in the risk of outbreak of war involving nuclear weapons,

Proceeding from the premise that the limitation of anti-ballistic systems, as well as certain agreed measures with respect to the limitation of strategic offensive arms, would contribute to the creation of more favorable conditions for further negotiations on limiting strategic arms,

Mindful of their obligations under Article VI of the Treaty on Non-Proliferation of Nuclear Weapons,

Declaring their intentions to achieve at the earliest possible date the cessation of the nuclear arms race and to take effective measures toward reductions in strategic arms, nuclear disarmament, and general and complete disarmament,

Desiring to contribute to the relaxation of international tension and the strengthening of trust between States, Have agreed as follows:

. . .

DONE at Moscow on May 26, 1972, in two copies, each in the English and Russian languages, both texts being equally authentic.

For the United States of America:

Richard Nixon
President of the United States of America.

For the Union of Soviet Socialist Republics:

L. I. Brezhnev
General Secretary of the central committee of the CPSU.

Today, outside the Warhead Assembly Building at the Nike site, "there is a rock garden (sand from the beach) and a plaque with the proficiency rating of this specific missile outfit: 97.1 is very good indeed. Rumor has it that this was the best missile team in the United States."

"The packing cases outside the building are containers which the various parts of the missile were shipped in to the area."

As with every prior military installation on the headlands, the Nikes eventually became obsolete. When Forts Barry and Cronkhite — land, buildings, installations, and all — were deeded by the army to the National Park Service, the remaining inert missiles became Park Service property.

Your Park Service ranger, by training and preference, may be a plant biologist, ornithologist, wild life expert, or Miwok Indian archeologist, but you ask him or her about the ownership of these missiles.

The one I spoke to replied: "Oh, sure. They're a national treasure. Just like the Liberty Bell!"

◆ ◆ ◆

As the smoke clears away, the gun crew carry another shell towards the breach of the gun.

"It's on its way, Sir!" and the shell from the 12-inch long range sea coast gun shoots 14 miles out to sea, the blast sending a gunner's hat flying.

HARBOR DEFENSES *in Action*

3798

● Plaster faces set to dry in former barracks, Fort Barry.

IN the fall of 1987 I interviewed **Col. Mervyn F. Burke** at his home in Berkeley. Col. Burke was born in 1899 and raised on the family farm in Santa Rosa.

Paul Metcalf — What did your family raise on the ranch?

Burke — We had pears, a few apples. Sold 'em to Chinamen.

    In 1916 he enlisted in the army. He celebrated his seventeenth birthday at Fort Barry.

Burke — I had just graduated from high school. I was the oldest of six kids.

PM — Had you always wanted to join the army?

Burke — No, no, never thought of it. Hoped to go to college, but there wasn't any money.

PM — When you enlisted, did you go right to Fort Barry?

Burke — Yes. Right from boot camp. I was only sixteen. I had to get my parent's consent in order to enlist. So I had to go home and sell the idea to my parents, and I turned out to be a pretty good salesman. They thought it would be a pretty good idea. One less mouth to feed, I think.

About seven or eight of us went to Fort Barry. And the only access to Barry then was by harbor boat. The only access. From the Presidio to Fort Scott, then to Fort Barry. And you had to hike up that cliff. Down below the lighthouse. They had a little flat car that would take the freight. That went straight up on the tracks, winched up at the top. You couldn't ride that. You had to walk up that cliff.

I immediately explored the possibilities of the library, on the top floor of Building 944. One of the fellows who had arrived with me, named Smith . . . he wasn't playing with a full deck. But he kept a card file of sorts, and he made copious notes. And he and I would be the only ones up in the library. What the hell he was studying I never found out. He was left-footed, he couldn't learn the foot drill. And I heard, after I had gone to Fort Miley, that he deserted.

There was another fellow that went with us — he was a Polack, and he had been a baker in civil life. Great big husky — I had first seen him at the recruiting station on Market Street when we were lined up to get our first shot — he was about three or four from me — and down he went in a dead faint. They dragged him up, revived him, gave him the shot anyway. He deserted, too. I've often wondered if either one of them were caught after war was declared, and the draft came along.

PM — That library that you talked about — was it a good library?

Burke — They were cast-offs — but I'd never seen them before, and they were interesting to me. They didn't help me much.

PM — As a young man fresh out of high school, did you find the army discipline onerous, or did you adapt to it easily?

Burke — No, I adapted without any trouble. I was a big green kid, and it was all so new to me. And, as the oldest of six kids, I was accustomed to family discipline. School was a discipline in those days, it wasn't a day-care center. When a parent said, do this, do that, you did it. When the teacher said, do this, do that, you did it.

PM — Tell me about target practice with the guns. What would you use for a target?

Burke — Oh, anything.

PM — A piece of canvas?

Burke — A rowboat, a sail — anything.

PM — How often was target practice engaged in?

Burke — Oh, about once or twice a year. This costs money. Remember, a soldier was getting $15 a month, with board and room. The army was on the shorts.

PM — What about fog, when you had target practice?

Burke — Oh, if it was foggy, you called it off.

PM — I recall reading that the original lighthouse at Point Bonita was up on high ground. They built the new one much lower, to try to get under the fog.

Burke — Well . . . you don't get under San Francisco fog.

PM — The men who worked the guns — what were their duties between those twice-a-year target practices?

Burke — Well, they had drills nearly every morning. And we had to police the joint. We didn't have any regular guard duty. Because, after all, there was only one company there at the time.

PM — It was almost like it was on standby.

Burke — Yeah. So that there was a permanent guard. We had two buglers, and they would alternate. One would be on duty twenty-four hours, and then twenty-four hours off. He blew all the calls. We didn't have reveille or retreat or anything like that. There was taps and lights out.

PM — Tell me about how the guns were aimed.

Burke — The gunner on the mortar — one would elevate and one would traverse, according to the information received from the observation point, which was out here (pointing to map, Point Bonita) on the point. Somehow or other they found out that I had a good telephone voice . . . and pretty soon they sent me out to the observation point, which was dug into the cliff — you can still see the ruins. We walked out, under the lighthouse, into this elaborate series of rooms, with the telescopes, the plotting board, and there was also the mine battery. The fellow with the azimuth could follow the target, and get a reading on what they called the T. I. bell, the time interval, which was a big bell that rang, say every thirty seconds. And he could read what his azimuth instrument said, which would be the angle from where he was. That was already laid out on the plotting board. And that fellow would triangulate it, another man would calculate, they would have to guess at the wind velocity, calculate the time of flight of shell, from the moment of firing to the moment of impact, and that would be the firing data to set the fuse. Then, when the bell rang in there, that had to be transmitted to the gun pit. And that was how they aimed the guns.

There was one man who was practically on permanent detail, on what they called the loading detail. This ammunition they used, in the gun itself, which would do the damage when it landed, it would age, and it had to be changed regularly. And he did that alone. Kept the powder in there, called Explosive D. . . . And it turned everything he wore green. Green eyebrows, green hair, uniform green.

You know, one of the biggest mysteries . . . for a long time I couldn't figure out how they got the big guns up into the emplacements. And it's still a bit of a mystery. The only solution, to me, is they were manufactured back East, of course, the emplacements were built by the engineers, all concrete — Battery Alexander, for example, Battery Mendell — then the barges had to take them from San Francisco, out through the gate, probably land them at the head of Rodeo Lagoon. Then they would be winched ashore, put on sleds, and dragged up Rodeo Lagoon Valley, and set in the emplacements.

PM — I read a story about one of those 16-inch guns being dragged through the tunnel, and getting stuck. I don't know if it's true or not.

Burke — Hmmm . . . I doubt it.

PM — It made good copy.

Burke — It made good copy.

PM — What was the army food like?

Burke — The army food to me was good. Always good. Because they were professionals. They had a mess sergeant who had studied. The ration was all in money, by Act of Congress. Each soldier was allowed one-tenth of an ounce of vinegar a day, one-fifteenth of an ounce of dry mustard a day, and so forth and so forth. The bread was baked, I think, at the bakery on Alcatraz. Baked by the federal prisoners. That went on for years. Alcatraz, at that time, was an army disciplinary barracks.

PM — You mentioned those two men who had gone A.W.O.L. Do you think that was peculiarities in their natures?

Burke — Well, they were older men. And they probably couldn't take the discipline, or the solitude. I don't know. I often wonder why they hell did they exist.

PM — Was there medical care at Fort Barry?

Burke (pointing at map) — This was the hospital. Just a two-bed, maybe three-bed — and I think they had a non-com there. The doctor would come over from Letterman at odd intervals, for short-arm inspection. In those days they didn't have any movies to scare the soldiers with; they had to be slides. And, believe me, the slides they showed us of syphilis and gonorrhea and so forth, that was enough to scare ya.

PM — Do you remember the name of the commanding officer when you were there?

Burke — Brown.

PM — What was your impression of him?

Burke — He was a stuffed shirt.

PM — What about the solitude, the isolation of the place? Did that seem to bother you, or bother the other men?

Burke — No, no. We didn't have any money to spend anyway. And you could get a weekend pass any time.

PM — Where did you go?

Burke — San Francisco. The most common source, of course, was the Barbary Coast.

PM — The harbor boat would take you?

Burke — Yes. You'd leave on the early morning boat, but then when you got off, you'd better get back by the late boat, or otherwise you walked. You had to walk over the hill from Sausalito. I've done that coming down from Santa Rosa. Walk up those steep steps from Sausalito to the top of the hill. There was a dairy ranch up there. The cows would scare you to death when they mooed. You came out by the rifle range.

There used to be a lot of wild lupin growing on the hill. The blue and yellow. I don't know if it's still there or not.

◇ ◇ ◇

Witten Harris, who lives in San Jose, got up at 4 A.M. one morning in the fall of 1987, and rode the bus to Fort Barry, to be interviewed by Marguerite Thayer. He came out again in the winter of 1988 and I talked to him.

Pfc. Harris was born in Bakersfield, California, in 1907. Finishing high school, age seventeen, he was unable to find work, so he joined the army. His first assignment was to a cavalry unit at Fort Bliss, Texas, and it was here he suffered his only disciplinary action, in ten years in the army: he was fined ten dollars and spent ten days in the guard house—for kicking his horse.

He was transferred to the Presidio in San Francisco in 1926, where he served as a stenographer. Together with the rest of his unit, he would come out to Fort Barry for two- and three-month stints, to practice marksmanship at the firing range. The men fired at targets, and the guns were 30.06, bolt action, ten shots at a time. He would shoot all day, until his shoulders were thoroughly sore. The range was usually 500 to 600 yards, although sometimes it was 300 yards, and he would shoot a whole clip in rapid fire. Pfc. Harris was classified as sharpshooter.

Describing the morning routine in the barracks, he said they would get up at 6:30 A.M., stand in formation for reveille, and eat breakfast perhaps half an hour later. A typical breakfast was S.O.S.* After

79

*Shit on a shingle: creamed chipped beef on toast.

good soldier, taking well to army life. For years his top sergeant was his best friend. He loved the isolation at Fort Barry, loved to hike over the hills, explore the batteries, etc. Asked what he did for entertainment, he said, "fish in the lagoon." "What did you catch in the lagoon?" "Cold. Never caught anything else."

He is enrolled now as a student at San Jose State University, working toward a degree in social science.

◇　◇　◇

Willis E. Spitzer came to the Headlands Center for the Arts in the fall of 1987, to be interviewed by Jennifer Dowley. He returned that winter, and I was able to talk to him.

Sgt. Spitzer was born in Bismarck, North Dakota, in 1917. As a young man in Bismarck, he was active in the National Guard. He moved to California in 1939, and when the National Guard mobilized, early in 1940, rather than return to his unit in North Dakota, he chose to enlist. He went first to the navy: "Give me the biggest guns you've got," he said. The recruiter did some research, and said, "Well, we've got one for you. An 18-inch, the biggest gun made." "Fine, where is it?" "Well, it's not in service. We decided we didn't need it, it's not really useful — so we're using it as ballast on a Red Cross ship." The next best bet turned out to be 16-inch guns on a battleship. Spitzer then went to the army, and the recruiter offered him 16-inch guns at Fort Cronkhite, outside San Francisco. Spitzer began to think that if war came along, it might be better to be on land than on a potential target floating in the ocean. He enlisted in the army.

Arriving at Fort Barry in mid-1940, he underwent training in small weapons, service guns, and later, 5 1/2-inch guns. Battery Townsley, with 16-inch guns, was newly completed, and was manned by only a small maintenance crew. Spitzer was assigned to Townsley, Battery E, late in 1940. He became part of the first crew to operate the guns.

"They didn't really know what to do with these big guns. Nobody knew much about them. They were navy guns, by the way — they were not army. Instead of putting them on a battleship, they put them up here with Coast Artillery. They were a new thing for the army. We were greatly understaffed, we only had 235 men to man those two big guns up there, which included the plotting room and the base end stations; and we were supposed to patrol the beach, and man the antiaircraft guns, on the hill up there. We were truly understaffed."

The crews started off with dry run target practice, just going through the motions. Spitzer's first position was in the plotting room,

breakfast, they would police the area, picking up cigarette butts, etc. Then to the rifle range.

To go anywhere meant going on foot. To go to the movies in San Francisco he would walk to Sausalito (through the tunnel), and take a military boat across the bay. For heavy transport at Barry, there were "big old chain-drive trucks" — Nash quads. And refuse from the barracks was taken to the incinerator, the other side of the lagoon, in a mule-driven wagon, driven by a mule skinner.

Except for the incident with his horse, Pfc. Harris was always a

● Witten Harris, qualified as a marksman on the Fort Barry rifle range, 1925.

working on the plotting board, but because of the shortage of men, he was shifted around, and soon was on the ammo detail, hauling in the powder and projectiles, through the tunnels. When they started live target practice, they would shoot once a month, firing at a piece of canvas perhaps five by six feet. This could be as much as thirty miles out, the outer limit of the gun's range. The guns were not really accurate at this range, although they *were* accurate up to nineteen miles. They would fire seven rounds on each gun, once a month. It cost the army $3,000 a round, and that didn't include the men. The gun used 664 pounds of TNT in the barrel, with a projectile that weighed 2,200 pounds. It took a little over a minute to travel nineteen miles, and the gun's recoil was thirty-five inches. "The sound wasn't sharp, it was more like an earthquake, like thunder, the ground shaking. A huge rumble. It would shake the whole mountain up there, believe me.

"It took a long time to train men on those guns up there. It wasn't an easy job at all, it just took a lot of training. You had to be precise all the time, you couldn't make mistakes. It took a crew of thirty-five to operate the gun, because you had to have a man for every move."

Spitzer was promoted to sergeant and became what was called a "key man," which meant that he was shifted daily from position to position, so as to become proficient in all of them. "One morning I would be in the plotting room, the next day they would shift me out to the base end station, the next time around they would put me in the gun crew, and one time they put me as gun pointer, who was the trigger man.

"When I worked in the plotting room, I had to figure the rotation of the earth, the waves, the tide, the wind at different levels, we always sent up a balloon to measure the wind; the projectile could go up as high as 45,000 feet before it would start back down again. And we had to figure the drift caused by different winds at different levels, the projectile going up and coming down again."

When the Japanese struck at Pearl Harbor, the men were completely surprised. They had thought there might be involvement in the war, but more likely with Germany.

Coastal defense became a sudden priority. Building 944 was immediately evacuated, and the company moved into Battery Townsley. The base end stations, the observation stations, had to be manned twenty-four hours a day, and rounding up and placing crews for these stations became Spitzer's responsibility. But two of the stations had been "lost" — they had been built and forgotten, nobody knew where they were. And they were well camouflaged. Spitzer and his crew drove and trudged up and down the coast, looking for wires,

talking to farmers, until they found them.

Then came the problem of manning them. Three men to a station, twenty-four-hour duty, no relief. Each station had folding bunks, no food, no water, no latrine. (Each soldier had a small shovel with which to dig a hole.) Spitzer was given a truck and a checkbook and spent the next several months driving up and down the coast, buying and hauling in food, water, temporary cook stoves to the various stations, and providing a couple of hours relief to a weary and glassy-eyed observer. Driving at night meant driving without headlights; the coast was blacked out. Once he was sent hurriedly to a station that could not be raised on the telephone: the entire crew had gone A.W.O.L.

Radar was introduced late in 1943 and was eventually installed in all of Battery Townsley's base end stations. Graduates from Radar School were brought in to train the men, and Spitzer was sent off to school, for just one week of training.

"The first time we used the radar, I was in one of the radar stations, tracking the target on the screen, and I caught holy hell for that, because the first round we fired, we sank the target and we spent $3,000 changing the target. The Colonel said, 'You're not supposed to *hit* the target!'"

Later, as the war in the Pacific expanded, experienced men were shipped out, and new men brought in. They were draftees—doing what they didn't want to do in a place they didn't want to do it. Spitzer had to train them.

Eventually, Sgt. Spitzer himself was shipped out, and he finished his service in the Pacific. He was discharged in December of 1945.

◇   ◇   ◇

Harry Peterson was interviewed in the fall of 1987 on videotape, for the Headlands Center for the Arts' archives. The interview took place in various rooms of Building 944, Fort Barry. I asked some questions, and made notes.

Corp. Peterson was born in 1918. He enlisted in the army in February 1941, for a one-year hitch, and was transferred to Fort Barry in June of that year — to Building 945. He was assigned as a gunner to "I" Battery, firing the six-inch guns at Battery Smith-Guthrie.

At that time, Buildings 944 and 945 each housed about 250 men. In the normal morning routine, the men would be awakened at 5:45 A.M. by a bugler and a sergeant. They would go to the parade ground for calisthenics, then into the mess hall for breakfast. This might be followed by close-order drill, and/or they would be marched to the

"I" Battery had an exceptional cook, a man who had cooked professionally for lumberjacks in the Pacific Northwest — and they had been a demanding crew. This cook tended to ignore the fussy army regulations, and cooked things his way. He did his own butchering, producing steaks where regulations called for roasts or hamburger. The bread was good, honest white bread, baked at the Presidio or Fort Scott, and brought in. The meals were all prepared on coal ranges. Strict observance of good table manners was enforced at mealtime. If you wanted your neighbor to pass you something, you said "please." If a serving dish was empty, you held it over your head, and a table waiter would collect it and replace it.

When he had a weekend pass, he would hitchhike on military vehicles to Fort Baker, then take a bus to San Francisco. There was a favorite bar where the guys all hung out.

When he was assigned to guard duty, he was normally given three rounds of ammunition. But in November 1941 — a month before Pearl Harbor — this was suddenly increased to 100 rounds, plus hand grenades. The military knew something.

On the morning of December 7, 1941, antiaircraft defense at Fort Barry consisted of four three-inch guns. (Many more were quickly brought in.) The barracks were immediately evacuated, and the men went to live in the batteries, squeezing in any way they could. They were expected to be capable of a five-minute response. Only the cooks remained in the barracks, preparing food and trucking it up to the men. Numerous check points, with sentries, were set up, between the tunnel and the batteries. All leaves and passes were either cancelled or greatly reduced. All enlistments were frozen — when Corp. Peterson had only forty days to go on his original hitch.

The men at Smith-Guthrie spent January and February of that winter building better living quarters, adjacent to the battery, doing much of the outdoor work in the rain.

Corp. Peterson remembers no case of venereal disease in Battery "I". And — (for this confidence, he requested that the audio and video be shut off) — he never saw evidence of men "fooling around," i.e., homosexuality.

Once, when on guard duty, Corp. Peterson brought in a soldier who had been arrested for raping a girl in Sausalito. From the army point of view, this was one of the most heinous crimes. Later, the guy hanged himself in his cell.

When Corp. Peterson finally received his discharge, his original one-year enlistment had stretched into four years, nine months, and twenty-three days. This is the sort of datum a soldier tends to remember.

battery. Corp. Peterson took part in many practice firings of the six-inch guns, shooting at sea-going targets.

In the sleeping quarters, there could be as many as seventy-five men to a room. Each man had a bunk and a foot locker. Every morning you had to sweep or mop under your bunk. Every Friday you washed the windows. There were occasional white-glove inspections for dust. Or the sergeant would bounce a quarter off your bunk sheet, to make sure it was perfectly tucked in.

Corp. Peterson liked the army food, but for a particular reason:

● Harry Peterson, gunner, "I" Battery, stationed at Fort Barry during World War II.

◇   ◇   ◇

In September of 1987 **Mario G. Paolini** (Col. AUS [Ret'd]) wrote saying that he would be glad to meet me and talk about the old days at the batteries. "My suggestion as to our meeting place is at the Battery position. Memories might be more readily stimulated and/or retrieved by the on-site visit."

Accordingly we met at the Alexander parking lot and walked the easy grade up to Battery Smith-Guthrie. By coincidence we were joined on this occasion by Corp. Peterson, Pfc. Kent Williams (see following), and the Headlands Center for the Arts video crew. The officer immediately took command.

Col. Paolini was an ROTC cadet in 1940. He graduated from Coast Artillery School, Fort Monroe, in February 1944, and was assigned to Smith-Guthrie Battery, Fort Barry. Arriving as a second lieutenant, he was promoted to first lieutenant, and became battery executive officer, Battery "I." During his stay here—nine months—he was quartered in the Smith Casemate, with the men.

The ammo in use at Smith-Guthrie, at the time of Pearl Harbor, dated from World War I, and was extremely unreliable. Coast Artillery, in the colonel's opinion, was already in decline, to be superseded by antiaircraft units.

To deceive the enemy aircraft, the battery at Smith-Guthrie was entirely covered by a permanent camouflage net, made of burlap. There was a sentry posted at the entrance, whose main duty, in actual practice, was to warn all and sundry of any approaching staff car.

The guns were regularly exercised with target practice. The methods of aiming were of three kinds: horizontal base system, vertical position-finding system, and self-contained system, with the first of these being most commonly used. Although more sophisticated, it broke down into essentially the same process described by Col. Burke, dating from 1916: triangulation, derived from trigonometry.

All the information came together in the Plotting Room, a low-ceilinged space, about twenty-one feet by twenty-four feet. These were six-inch guns, and in the aiming process allowance had to be made for wind, air density, heat of powder, and drift (a shell travels in a spiral, like a football, and tends to drift in the same way). At Battery Townsley, where sixteen-inch guns were fired, allowance was also made for the earth's rotation: a shell of this size becomes, in effect, a satellite.

Prior to firing, the projectile must be rammed perfectly into the gun, to ensure accuracy. Mechanical rammers were tried, but they

83

● "I" Battery trained lion and mascot.

proved to be less efficient than the old-fashioned manual method.

At each firing, the gun sergeant must listen to hear the primer go off.

Every firing required that two men stand in such a position that each had one ear exposed to the full noise of the blast, and there was considerable ear damage. Col. Paolini's company happened to contain two men who were already deaf. Since no further damage could be done to their ears, they regularly received these assignments.

Firing practice was held both day and night, with powerful searchlights for the night firings. If the fog came in, there was no

practice—the assumption being that any attacking enemy would be equally inhibited.

Radar arrived in the spring of 1942, but it was a closely guarded secret, and was not put into use at once. There were actually two men at Smith-Guthrie who had graduated from Radar School, a fact that was not revealed.

Col. Paolini's company included a sergeant who had been an animal trainer in civilian life, and he brought in a couple of baby lions, for pets. The Battery "I" baseball team, playing on what is now the Alexander parking lot, was known as the Barry Lions.

After the war, the Japanese submarine commander whose order to shell San Francisco had been rescinded, visited the city, introduced himself to Mayor Christopher, reminded him of how close he had come to giving the city a Christmas present.

The planning of the attack for Christmas was not accidental; surprise military moves are frequently made on holidays or Sundays.

◇　◇　◇

Kent Williams sent me a written memoir of his stay at Fort Barry. Later he visited, and we toured several of the buildings and fortifications.

Pfc. Williams was drafted into the army in 1952. He took basic training at Fort Ord, and, following an aptitude test, he was assigned to Fort Barry for combat military police training. He arrived in February 1953—during the Korean War. He was twenty-two years old.

"Our training started almost immediately. This consisted, in part, of qualifying on the Departmental rifle range with riot shotguns, Army Colt M1911A .45 automatics and .30 cal. 'burp' or 'grease' guns.

"We were kept on a short chain. There were only two places we could go individually on our own—the orderly room each evening before chow for our mail and occasionally to the Fort Barry theatre to the movies. We were marched everywhere else. There were four platoons in each building, 944 and 945. I was in 945, fourth platoon, third floor, east end. About thirty-five of us comprised each platoon. The day started at 5 A.M., being awakened via the 'bitch box'—an intercom system wired to each platoon controlled from the orderly room—with records by Glenn Miller, Benny Goodman, Tommy Dorsey, etc., played at FULL volume. The cadremen ran down the halls into our rooms yelling 'Is everybody happy?' We bailed out of our sacks and dressed rapidly in order to assemble in front of each building to be double-timed down the hill in the dark to the 'Y' at

● Kent Williams, trained as MP during the Korean War, stationed at Fort Barry.

six feet high by eight feet square from which our PE instructor put us through our 'Army Daily Dozen' collection of exercises including squat-jumps, push-ups, etc.

"About once a week we went to the Ft. Baker parade ground for a 'round-robin' of come-alongs wherein we threw each other and in turn got thrown. We were supposed to have learned by now how to 'fall' without busting our bones. This didn't always work according to plan.

"After dinner was spent in cleaning weapons, spit shining boots and shoes, and polishing brass. The day ended at 9:30 with lights out.

"One night shortly after our arrival the whole troop in 945 was called out to assemble outside the front door to be addressed by the company cook on how cuisine-wise, to be fair to our fellow soldiers. Being on the fringe of our large group I couldn't see the head chef, who had a deep, raspy voice like Andy Devine. . . .

"'Youse guys is fuckin' yer buddies. Take ONE pork chop, see? If you take two pork chops and don't eat 'em, yer fuckin' yer buddy, unnerstan'? If youse wants another pork chop, come back with yer tray empty, see, an' I'll prob'ly give ya one, see? But don't go fuckin' yer buddy, okay?'

"This diatribe went on for what seemed like half an hour. I stood smoking a cigarette, watching the insects flutter around the glare from the big clear glass light bulb in the porch ceiling, listening to his voice rasp out through the night and wondering if this was really for real."

Following his discharge from the army, Kent Williams has become something of a military buff, and he often comes to visit Forts Barry and Cronkhite. On the first such visit, he was amazed to discover old batteries and fortifications, along the coast. During his enlistment he had never known they were there — so restricted had his movements been.

◆ ◆ ◆

85

Bunker Rd. and back to our barracks and given our breakfast schedule — first and third platoons first or whatever — and received at the same time orders on the uniform of the day, which varied as to the days activity — field or classroom and, of course, the weather. If you ate first you went directly to the messhall. If you were on the second feeding shift you made your bunk, prepared your uniform and equipment and 'shit, showered, and shaved.'"

"As future MP's, it was drummed repeatedly into us to use 'only that force which is necessary' in dealing with belligerent prisoners or intractable drunks, etc. To this end we were grilled on the UCMJ — Uniform Code of Military Justice — and trained in the army version of martial arts commonly called 'come-alongs.' [If a man comes at you with a gun or a knife, you duck under his arm, grasp him by the forearm near the shoulder, and fling him over your back to the ground.] This we did on thin mats on the floor of the gym above the bowling alley across from the Ft. Barry theatre. I learned just enough of this to get my neck broken if I ever tried it for real, which I never did.

"At the end of the training day we marched to the Ft. Barry parade ground (then beautifully maintained) on which there was one item only — at the west end — a white painted wooden platform about

● Former barracks, now art center. Building 944, Fort Barry.

86

● Remains of rescue boat pier, Bonita Cove.

"MARCH 5, 1853, a sunny Saturday, found the steamer *Tennessee*, a big three-masted sidewheel steamship, approaching the end of a twenty-one-day journey from Panama. She was Pacific Mail's proudest, 1,350 tons, and had been shuttling between Gate and Isthmus for almost three years. Her 551 passengers were excited, for the gate and the port of gold were only 100 miles away."

The S.S. *Tennessee* had been purchased by the Pacific Mail Steamship Company in 1849, to add to their fleet of steamers running a shuttle service between the Isthmus of Panama and San Francisco, carrying in gold-seekers, and bringing out gold.

There are accounts of one of her earlier voyages — 1850:

"*Tennessee* was so crowded on her first voyage to San Francisco that twenty steerage passengers were unable to obtain berths. These unfortunates slept on deck; 'the purser has meted out an old mainsail for them. . . .'"

" . . . It is curious to walk over the deck at night; men are lying about in every place large enough to hold them; hammocks are swung across the vessel and fastened to every stanchion and rope. . . . "

Food, however, at least for the cabin passengers, was excellent:

"Turkey, Goose, Duck, Beef, Pork, Lamb & Kid all fresh, Beef, Ham, Pork & Fish salted, Raisins, Prunes, Almonds, Filberts, Preserves, Tea, Coffee, Loaf Sugar, Pies, Puddings, Cakes, Cheese, Butter, Sardines, Green Peas, Green Corn, Green Beans, Pickles, Oranges, Bananas, Hot Cakes, Honey, Jams, Buckwheats, Eggs, Omelets, &c, &c. . . . "

"Meals in steerage were of lesser quality. . . . Each passenger approached the bar with tin pot and pan in hand and was served salt beef, duff (a boiled pudding made from suet, flour, and dried fruit), coffee or soup. He then 'plants himself down where he can eat it.'"

"Among the passengers were 'twelve or fourteen women of bad character' and 'a little knot of gamblers, with their women. . . . Every night the gamblers opened a faro bank in their cabin. . . .'"

At the same time: "With the large number of clergy on board, regular religious services offered an alternative. . . . "

The voyage in 1853 did not begin auspiciously:

"In transferring the passengers on board, — all in such a tremendous rush and hurry, you know, to get that crowd on in a few hours, — one or two fell into the water; and the chief mate, Dowling, Richard Dowling, — jumped straight over and after them. It was a courageous thing to do, under the circumstances, for that bay is full of sharks, and it was only by chance that he got the passengers out and got back alive."

There was a stop at Acapulco, but few of the passengers went ashore, "for fear of the Isthmus fever."

There was already illness on board, "brought on by passengers who had caught yellow fever while waiting for the ship in Panama. As with other voyages, the fever began to take a toll. Dealing with the fever and the resultant deaths had never become commonplace with the ship's surgeon, Dr. Alex McNaughton. Having successfully quelled outbreaks of the fever on board *Tennessee* in the past, McNaughton had eventually fallen into despair with each repetition of sickness and death. In January of 1853, McNaughton, facing yet another outbreak on board, and 'losing his first cases, and seeing the terror spread around him, soon became demoralized, losing sleep, resorted to stimulants, and finally arrived at such a condition that his brother officers felt it necessary to put him in irons. He was, in fact, a maniac.' Through the efforts of several passengers, the spread of the disease was halted and many of the stricken recovered. Dr. McNaughton also apparently recovered, for the next month he was back on board the *Tennessee* for her last voyage. Once again, though, the fever struck, and McNaughton snapped. Halfway through the voyage to San Francisco he slit his throat. Fortunately, he was discovered and survived. . . . "

On the final night of *Tennessee's* final voyage, fog closed in, and in the morning it was still thick. "Captain Mellus, confident of his position, began to slowly work the ship toward the Golden Gate. Meanwhile, some of the passengers, confident of a delay, made their way below deck to start on breakfast. The strong current of the gate caught the ship, and unknown to the Captain, slowly began to swing the *Tennessee* past the harbor entrance and along the rocky shoreline of the Marin County coast. The first inkling of disaster came a little after nine o'clock, when a steerage passenger who had been standing at the bow ran towards the wheelhouse, shouting that he could see breakers ahead. By this time Mellus could hear the crashing waves, and as the fog suddenly lifted, the narrow confines of a sand beach could be seen; behind the ship, and surrounding the *Tennessee*, were the jagged spires of bare rock. At that moment, the ship struck."

"We sat down . . . and called for something to eat, when there came an awful crash of the steamer. Everybody knew instantly that we'd struck. Everything went off the table in a heap. . . . "

"She struck kind of sidelong, grazed the reef, and slid off. We saw the cliff ahead, tried to back off, and the surf threw the stern around, so that a rock, which the captain had taken for Miles Rock, was right at our stern, and prevented us from backing. Then the surf kept driving her in, and she struck nearly broadside on, and the swell carried her over till she stuck on the reef, and there she was fixed. . . . "

" . . . Each wave pounded her closer to the shore and deeper into the sand. The decks were filled with milling passengers, many of whom were crying and screaming. Some began to pray as the rocking of the ship began incessantly tolling the ship's bell. 'The women took it for the toll of doom.'"

"It was a providential landing in a place of bold bluffs and smashing waves." (About two miles north of Point Bonita). "Indian Cove, they called it up to that time, — and the cove was so narrow that fifty feet from the stern, or fifty feet from the ship's nose, would have brought us on the cliffs. . . . "

Today, it is Tennessee Cove, with Tennessee Beach, Tennessee Point, and Tennessee Valley.

"Well, this same chief mate Dowling, that jumped overboard at Panama Bay, watched his chance, and took a small line, — fastened about his body, — and jumped overboard on one of the high seas. He was carried ashore and thrown upon the rocks, and happened by good luck to be able to get hold of something and hang on when the undertow went back, and then managed to scramble up out of reach of the water. So then they sent a larger line over, and then a cable hawser, from the wheelhouse, and three or four other men went over."

Tom Gihon, the express messenger, "got the steward to help him, and they got a quarter-boat down, on their own responsibility, and he found he could get the ladies ashore, so a few of the passengers that hadn't anything to do turned in and helped him, and finally he got them all safe to the beach. It took half the day, — O, 'twas a tremendous job. He had to threaten to kill the men if they didn't keep back, — they would have rushed right over the women and children and piled into the boat. . . . "

Searching the ship for any strays, he found a Miss Sanford in her cabin.

"'Hurry up!'

"'Why, what's the matter?' says she.

"He said, 'The vessel's ashore!'

"She said, 'I *thought* it was queer that the steamer went bumping that way through the Gate.'

"She was getting everything together, just as methodical as a Yankee school-marm would, you know."

"All this time the ship's bell kept tolling a terrible toll . . . Of course there was no life-saving station then, and almost no settlements in Marin County. . . . "

"The officers had given up trying to save the ship and they had to hurry before the cabins filled with water, to get the bedding out of the berths. They had them take that and all the sails, and get it all ashore and take hold and make tents for the people. . . . "

"It was foggy, cold weather, and hundreds of people crowded on the little beach. . . . "

The surgeon, who had gone crazy and slit his throat, was brought ashore, and a place was made for him.

" . . . A great many of the steerage passengers got guides from those who had been in the country before, and started off across the mountains to walk to Sausalito." When word of the wreck reached the Sausalito people, "Old Captain Richardson was the first one to come — the same man after whom Richardson Bay was named. His house was at Sausalito, and he was a regular old-timer; had his ranch there in Mexican times."

"As the workers frantically stripped the steamer it began to go to pieces in the surf." " . . . Her back broken, butt ends started and bottom probably bilged. . . . " "Around noon on March 8, the hull split, and 'all that heavy machinery went right down through the bottom' as the engine tore free of its timber mounts and broke apart."

Of the 551 passengers on board, and all the officers and crew, not a single life was lost.

Captain Mellus was blamed for the wreck, "for he ought not to have tried to make the gate in that fog without more care. It appeared that the *Sierra Nevada* could be seen going in ahead of us, and we had followed her: Mellus didn't want the opposition boat to go in ahead and report we were outside. Then the fog came down. . . . "

Today, 135 years later, a severe storm will occasionally expose a fragment — a pulley block, or some such — of the *Tennessee*.

March 6, 1853, was the date of the wreck. Three days earlier — March 3 — Congress had appropriated $25,000 for construction of a lighthouse at Point Bonita. (*Punta de Bonetes* was the original name — because the rock formation resembled a Spanish cleric's three-cornered hat.)

In April of 1855 the first lighthouse opened, sending its light from high on the cliff above the point, and in August of that year a fog cannon was added, with a lonely Sgt. Edward Maloney to man it. "His instructions were to fire that gun every half-hour whenever the fog obscured the entrance to the Bay. He wrote to the lighthouse service two months later, 'I cannot find any person here to relieve me, not five minutes; I have been up three days and nights, had only two hours' rest — I was nearly used up. All the rest I would require in the twenty-four hours is two, if only I could get it.'"

It soon became apparent that the lighthouse high on the cliff was useless in fog, and, in 1872, a new signal was constructed at the eastern end of Point Bonita, "a promontory of unbelievable thinness and delicacy under which the sea roars and tunnels completely through. This finger of black-brown rock thrusts out from Marin County for half a mile. At one point it is only as thick as a man's outspread arms and at another it recently disappeared altogether and has been replaced by a 165-foot suspension footbridge. Although its western or weather face takes the sea's brunt, its laughingly-styled lee face is also heavily battered. Outgoing tides and constant eddies gnaw at it. In present time the approach to the lighthouse out on the end was narrowed by erosion to a shelving trail, scarcely three feet wide, scratched along a thundering drop of 100 feet."

In 1875 this tortuous path was replaced by a tunnel, 118 feet long, dug or blasted through solid rock. And two years later the fog signal was replaced by the present lighthouse, at the point.

Before modern automation, the lightkeeper and his family lived close by. Food provisions arrived perhaps four times a year, and the meagre diet was supplemented by wild berries and wild mushrooms. (The test for the mushrooms was to throw a dime in the frying pan: if the dime turns black, the mushrooms are poisonous; if it remains shiny, they're safe.)

Cabbages were also planted on the steep cliffs along the pathway. Their descendents, reverting to a genetically wild state, survive today.

"1967 — Coast Guard Officer Joe Belisle reports waves 130 feet high crashing over top of lighthouse."

"On January 30, 1864, the barque *Jenny Ford* left San Francisco for Puget Sound to load lumber. Unfortunately the vessel sailed too close to shore, and was carried ashore at Bird Rock by heavy seas."

" . . . The wrecking schooner *Samson* which was anchored off Point Bonita removing iron plates from the wrecked steamer *City of New York* . . . went adrift and was carried north, around the point, where she stranded on rocks. . . ."

● Point Bonita lighthouse and suspension bridge.

". . . the steel barges *Agattu* and *Kona*, laden with explosives, chlorine, lumber, and other assorted goods, went adrift after being towed out of the Golden Gate by tugs enroute to Hawaii. Storm winds and waves swept the barges ashore near Bird Rock, *Kona* breaking in two and sinking in the small cove below and *Agattu* grounding on Rodeo Beach."

"Alaska Miners Drowned Near Golden Gate — *Helen W. Almy* capsizes and forty Men are Missing."

". . . Daring rescue of passengers from the steamer *Eureka* which was carrying 2 tons of dynamite."

"In 1854 the clipper *San Francisco*, a fine ship from New York on her maiden voyage, with cargo valued at $400,000, was beating through the entrance when she struck rocks on the north side. . . . As soon as word came of the clipper's plight, plunderers were at the scene by every small craft that would float. Some two hundred of them, 'nearly all armed with the usual weapons, five or six-shooters and bowie knives . . . stood their ground and continued to take and rob as they pleased' — until a storm blew up, when some of the pirate boats capsized and drowned a dozen on the spot or swept them out to sea."

"Recognizing the need for experienced assistance to save lives and property at ship wrecks, Congress authorized on June 18, 1878, the establishment of the Life-Saving Service under the supervision of general superintendent."
And: " . . . Congress authorized the establishment of Point Bonita Life-Saving Station on the north shore in 1898. . . . "

"Most of the crews turned out to be Scandinavian immigrants — Danes, Swedes, and Norwegians — who had learned about the sea from years as deep water sailors. Discipline at the stations commonly was very strict, requiring sober behavior (no liquor permitted at the stations) and clean, orderly habits. The four-hour beach patrols were arduous during high winds and cold weather."
Captain Nelson: "It is a common occurrence to be capsized. I have a method that never fails of testing the mettle of a man. As you know, when rowing the men have their backs to the front of the boat and cannot see what lies ahead of them. If a man turns his head when he hears a fussing of the water behind him, he is not the man for our work. By turning his head he takes five pounds of effort off his oar at the moment when every pound counts. I pay him off as soon as we reach the beach."

"In the late 1890s the Service introduced the 2000-pound, thirty-foot Dobbins lifeboat which not only weighed more than the earlier lifeboat models, making it more difficult to capsize in the breakers, but which also quickly righted and bailed itself after over-turning."

"In 1909 the Life-Saving Service began introducing power lifeboats to its stations."
Today, most of the work is done by helicopters. . . .

On the outer coast, just north of Point Bonita, lies a dangerous shoal called Potato Patch, "so called not because the almost constant whitecaps over it resembles mashed potatoes but because in the old days schooners carrying sacks of potatoes from Bodega Bay sometimes lost their cargos while crossing it."
"When the winter swells roll in from the far Pacific and thunder into churning white at the bar," the mariners would say, "the bar is breaking. . . . "
Or if the Potato Patch churned into a particularly violent froth, it might mean that killer whales — Orca — were attacking the migrating California Grey. . . .

◆　◆　◆

103

● Fruit tree planted long ago by farmers, Oakwood Valley.

AT one time there was a considerable Portuguese population in rural Marin. The men came first, not from Portugal, but from the Azores. According to Jack Tracy, they were "Catholic, uneducated, and did not speak English." They came as volunteers or stowaways on Yankee whalers that had put into the Azores for wood and water, and they were escaping a twenty-year enlistment in the *British* army — this being the result of a debt owed by the king of Portugal to the king of England. The whalers would put into Sausalito harbor, again for wood and water, and the Portuguese would jump ship, disappearing into the pastoral landscape of Marin in order to become and remain anonymous — because they were illegal aliens. (It was a pattern established earlier by the Chinese coolies, who were brought in as cheap labor, on temporary visas, and simply stayed on.)

The Portuguese found jobs, worked hard, began to lease land (from Samuel Throckmorton among others) on which to establish dairy farms. They sent back to the Azores for their women, whom they married, and the children of these unions were legal American citizens. Eventually the mothers and fathers were quietly accepted, although their status was not legally clarified until the 1930s.

Another landowner from whom dairy farms were leased, and perhaps bought, was a mysterious figure named Anton Borel, Swiss consul in San Francisco, and a man of means. A 1906 map shows that the central portion of the headlands, from Rodeo Lagoon eastward, consisted of 2,208.64 acres, all of which belonged to Borel. It was divided into Lots A, B, and C, each comprising a dairy farm. Houses, barns, creamery, and springs are clearly marked on the map.

Rodeo Valley and Rodeo Lagoon trace their names to the roundup of cattle from the grazing lands that was held annually in the valley.

The Portuguese brought with them from the Azores the tradition of the Chama Rita festival:

"The history of the festival dates back to 1296. At that time the Kingdom of Portugal under King Diniz and Queen Isabel was being swept by a severe famine. The Queen, who was later sainted, prayed for the relief of her suffering people. As in all legends based on fact, it is believed that ships laden with supplies did indeed arrive after this and the famine was subdued.

At a church outside Lisbon, in the Village of Alemquer, Queen Isabel called for a High Mass and proclaimed a festival for the populace to rejoice. It is said that while she prayed, the Holy Ghost descended in the form of a dove. For this reason, the crown of Isabel, which is worn each year by the Queen

of the Chama Rita, supports a dove with outspread wings."

In the early days of the Portuguese in Marin, "the Holiday Season began with a cattle drive which started from Bolinas, on the ocean side of the coastal range, and wound its way along the trails and roads to Sausalito. Ranchers along the way donated calves for the auction, and Portuguese cowboys, dressed in their finest riding clothes, picked up cattle as they moved toward Sausalito. On the trail they decorated the animals with ribbons, bells and flowers for the gala entry into town."

The cattle were auctioned for charity, and the festival climaxed with feasting (*sopa, carne e vino*) and dancing.

Chama Rita translates as "Please dance with me," with a courtly emphasis on *please* — an emphasis perhaps untranslatable in other Romance languages.

◇ ◇ ◇

Casius Eugene Poole visited the Headlands Center for the Arts in the winter of 1988, to offer his reminiscences.

Mr. Poole was born in Ukiah, California, in 1918, and his family moved to Sausalito a year later. As a child, he was friendly with the children of Captain Dillon, who was posted at Fort Barry with the Coast Artillery, and he also became friendly with Sam Silva, dairy farmer, and his family. He grew up with the Marin Headlands as his childhood playground.

"When we were kids we'd climb over the hill and come down the canyon by Sam Silva's ranch. We'd go down to the beach and hunt for agates. Then we'd come by the ranch again, and we'd always have milk to drink. Sam always let us drink all the milk that we wanted to. Us kids used to really drink that

milk, after being out there at the beach all day. We loaded ourselves. Generally we'd hike up the canyon, but when we had a belly full of milk, we went up the dirt road. We just couldn't take it, hiking up that steep hill like that, with all that milk in us.

"The reason Sam was always good to us, I mean, we weren't destructive kids, and we'd find his calves stuck down in the creeks, and us kids would always pull the calves out of the creek. And he always appreciated that."

I asked him if he remembered the annual Portuguese festival of Chama Rita.

"I remember, I remember. I was just old enough to remember. . . . You see, out on Coloma, at the corner of Coloma and Tamales, they still have the corral out there where they used to bring the cows. From there they would parade the cows up to the church. And they were blessed and everything. And then they would bring them back, and they were butchered, and the Portuguese people would get a certain amount of meat. They still do it to this day, only they don't parade the cattle. They have their festivities and dancing."

He spoke again about the ranch country:

"Well, it was a wonderful place for us kids out there. We'd come over the hills, we used to have our bows and arrows and that, our greatest sport was chasing the pack rats, they'd come out of their nests and we'd try to shoot 'em with bow and arrow. And you know that creek, that comes up by the rifle range? Well, there used to be steelhead going up and down through there; oh, that was always a wonderful steelhead stream. We used to chase 'em up and down the creek."

I asked him about horseback riding:

"Well, I've rode horses all my life, as far back as I can remember. Up here at the top of the hill, by KDFC Radio Station, up to the left, there used to be about ten horses up there that belonged to somebody, and I used to snitch my mother's carrots, and I'd take the carrot. There was a nice white horse up there, and I'd feed him the carrot, and hop on his back and go for a ride, ride Indian style, just grab the mane, and just ride. These horses were just in the pasture up there, and I never did know who they belonged to. That used to be a great pastime for me."

I asked him if he was ever a hunter:

"Oh, yes, we used to hunt — this is one of the best quail and cottontail hunting areas that were right here. Well, and here's another thing, the reason why there was a lot of cottontail and jackrabbits and quail was because us kids used to kill the bobcats. So, consequently, you're talking about nature's balance, us kids was more or less kinda making, I don't know if it was an off balance or not, but it was a balance to the point that there was a lot of quail and a lot of cottontail, they were running all over the place. But to this day, I ride my horse, and I cannot see a cottontail; it's very, very rare that I see a cottontail. I do see quail, but not like I used to. I see the jackrabbit, but not like there used to be.

"And before it became the Golden Gate National Recreation Area, Sam Silva's ranch there was a hunting club. I did not belong to it, they called it the Golden Gate Hunting Club. I hunted my deer on the other side of the fence, what they chased over I got.

"You know it was fortunate, when us kids were growing up and that, we were very fortunate to have a place where we could go and hunt and be right in our back yard. But it seems like now today, kids can't do hardly anything, you can't do this, you can't do that, you can't go here, you can't go there. . . ."

Mr. Poole talked about a whiskey still that operated in Tennessee Valley, during prohibition. "And it was one of the most beautiful

mushroom fields that you ever could get to, we used to go in there and get mushrooms and take 'em into town to the stores and they would buy the mushrooms, they were so nice." To make sure they were getting the right kind, "We only took the ones that showed pink."

The still was destroyed by the law, but there was more activity at the beach: "See, these rum runners would go out to the mother ship and pick up a load of booze. Well, they would come into Tennessee Beach, and they would stay off just the other side of the breakers, and this friend of mine used to swim ashore with a rope so that he could pull the bottles of whiskey which were all wrapped up in tules — and, you know, tules will float — so they were in sacks of about four, and they would float ashore. And they would truck it out of there."

In Sausalito harbor: "We used to see these speed boats, and you could see the machine guns, and, you know, being kids and you're always snooping around, and they're not paying too much attention. . . ."

◇   ◇   ◇

 Miwok trail from the old cistern above Silva ranch, Gerbode Valley.

Bret Harte, *The Legend of Devil's Point*: "On the northerly shore of San Francisco Bay, at a point where the Golden Gate broadens into the Pacific stands a bluff promontory. It affords shelter from the prevailing winds to a semi-circular bay on the east. Around this bay the hillside is black and barren, but there are traces of former habitation in a weather-beaten cabin and deserted corral. It is said that these were originally built by an enterprising squatter, who for some unaccountable reason abandoned them shortly after. The 'Jumper' who succeeded him disappeared one day, quite as mysteriously. The third tenant, who seemed to be a man of sanguine, hopeful temperament, divided the property into building lots, staked off the hillside, and projected the map of a new metropolis. Failing, however, to convince the citizens of San Francisco that they had mistaken the site of their city, he presently fell into dissipation and despondency. He was frequently observed haunting the narrow strip of beach at low tide, or perched upon the cliff at high water. In the latter position a sheep-tender one day found him, cold and pulseless, with a map of his property in his hand, and his face turned toward the distant sea."

A later account: "Just north of the first high ridge of the Marin Headlands, between the Golden Gate Cliffs and the foothills of Mount Tamalpais, is the place called Rodeo Valley. . . .

"In this valley, in 1966, work actually began on what was to be a city of 18,000 inhabitants. The name of that city was to be Marincello."

The name a promoter's wedding of Marin and Monticello. "Glossy drawings and three-dimensional models showed a city unlike anything this largely suburban county had seen. In its original version Marincello would have housed, on the rugged 2,100 acre site, some 30,000 people.

"At the summit of the city, at the highest point in the Headlands, would rise a 'landmark hotel.'

"'Our goal is to make Marincello the most beautiful planned community in the world.'

"On November 12, 1965 . . . the Board of Supervisors of Marin County approved the Marincello master plan.

"But . . . a few stubborn workers were joining together to continue to oppose the project.

"Men and machines arrived to reshape the hidden valley. A wide access boulevard was laid out. Underground conduits were dug for utility lines. A pair of handsome stucco entry gates were built leading to nothing."

The developer — Thomas Frouge — "could not, after all, carry out certain financial agreements made with Gulf Oil and with another partner. A legal tangle followed that lasted three long years."

Meanwhile, "the climate of opinion was shifting steadily against their common project. . . . Early backers grew doubtful or changed sides."

"On January 5, 1969, the remarkable man named Thomas Frouge died in New York.

"On December 22, 1972, Gulf sold its land in the Headlands to the Nature Conservancy. The conservancy shortly conveyed it to the National Park Service. And the story of Marincello was done."

◆ ◆ ◆

● The model of Marincello, preserved in irony by the Park Service.

108

● Pampas grass: headlands exotic.

A rich variety of vegetation may be found in the Marin Headlands, a wealth that may be traced to three causes: (1) the variety of soils produced by the faults and other geological formations; (2) the Mediterranean climate, with wet winters and dry summers; and (3) the variety of topography. There are some plants that grow in the Marin Headlands and nowhere else.

The original ground cover consisted of Coastal Prairie, or Perennial Grasslands — and Coastal Scrub. There were also Dunes, Riparian Lands, and Oak Woodlands.

Whatever the terms, the headlands are found in isolation between two distinct floristic zones, with Hard Chaparral to the south, and Redwoods to the north. And, most students will agree, "no one has been quite able to successfully categorize the plant community of the Headlands; it is unique to California.

"In the primitive Marin landscape, the natural mosaic of woods, grass and brush was maintained by two factors: grazing (originally by elk), and occasional wildfire. The native plants of our woods and brushfields are adapted, to some degree, to both." In addition, the Indians annually burned the grasslands—to find game, seeds, and acorns.

Native flowers and other plants that may be found in the headlands, according to location and season, include:
Footsteps of Spring.
Hog Fennel, Hound's Tongue, Mule Ears, Hen-and-Chickens, Sticky Monkeyflower.
Baby Blue-eyes, Tidy Tips, Milk Maids, Blow Wives.
Slinkpod, Coastal Sage, Sedges, and Rushes.
Zigadene.
Farewell to Spring.

When Don Guillermo Antonio Richardson acquired his Rancho Saucelito in 1841, he imported some Mexican cattle, and they brought with them Mexican grass seeds, stuck in their fur and hair. These took root and spread, replacing some of the native grasses.

This may have been the first of what has come over the years to be an onslaught of invasion.

The first farmers, Portuguese and others, looked on the grasslands as being perfect for cattle — but the heavy grazing badly damaged the perennials. Accordingly, annual grasses were imported from Mediterranean sources. Other seeds arrived in cattle droves, old mattresses, however. Today the original grasses survive only in isolated areas.

" . . . Big chunks of parkland are being taken over by plants that never belonged in

113

● Seeds found on a walk through Oakwood Valley: oak, eucalyptus, cypress.   ● Eucalyptus invading native oak, Oakwood Valley.

And the aptly named freeway daisy ("very destructive").

Many of the invading exotics had for centuries enjoyed a stable niche in the ecology of their homelands. Arriving in the headlands, without the constraints of familiar competition, they have run wild.

The eucalyptus has become a modern fire hazard. The brush beneath the tree is highly inflammable, and the green wood contains a chemical that ignites quickly. A eucalyptus grove, once burned over, recovers quickly. "Fuel loads will continue to accumulate until a severe wildfire occurs which could destroy large natural and developed areas."

Many feel that some of the most offensive exotics — eucalyptus, pampas grass, the bromes, freeway daisy — should be eradicated if possible, or at least severely controlled. The extent to which such measures may — or should — be undertaken, is a matter of ongoing controversy.

◇   ◇   ◇

The sea otter, long ago hunted out by the Aleuts in their bidarkas, has departed the rocky Marin shoreline and the Farallons, moving his range southward. But other marine mammals remain, among them the California sea lion, the northern elephant seal, and the Pacific harbor seal, with haul-out sites and rookeries on sandy beaches and rock terraces.

Among these, the California sea lion is certainly the most vocal, the noisiest, "one of the most vocal of all mammals, marine or otherwise." Even in the act of nursing, "suckling is surprisingly noisy." The eyes of the sea lion are small and dark, "adapted for clear vision in and out of the water." The male will grow to 600 or 700 pounds, and up to seven feet in length.

the old scene. Of these, the brooms, French and Scotch, are the most virulent. Spreading outward from towns and roads, they colonize whole hillsides."

Imported plants and trees are called "exotics," and prime among them is the eucalyptus tree. Entrepreneurs — one of whom, reportedly, was the writer Jack London — introduced eucalyptus from Australia in the 1850s, thinking they could sell it for building houses, making furniture, almost anything. The trees were planted as shade for cattle and houses, and as windbreaks. Fast-growing and fast-spreading, invading the diminishing oaklands, they proved to be useless as structural wood. It seems some 200 species of eucalyptus are native to Australia, and the one chosen to import, the blue gum, was the wrong one.

Other exotics include:

Pampas grass, imported from South America, a "pest," pushing out other vegetation.

Monterey pine and cypress.

Ice plant, dandelion, smartweed.

Poison hemlock, ripgut brome.

● Bobcat specimen from a collection of native animals, classroom at the Headlands Institute.

The northern elephant seal is the giant of the tribe. "The adult male may grow to over 16 feet in length and over 6,000 pounds." The female gives birth on dry land, and "the pup nurses for about 25 days, generally gaining about 10 pounds a day. After the nursing period, the mother returns to the sea (she has been out of the water and not feeding for about 2 months)." Back in deep water, "it is thought that Elephant Seals are solitary when at sea."

As you walk along the beach, don't be surprised to see a head — "round, cat-like" — and a pair of eyes — "large and dark" — emerging from the water, just offshore. They belong to the harbor seal, and they will seem to follow you, watching, as you walk.

When William A. Richardson acquired his Rancho Sauselito in 1841, the land was home to varieties of wild game, such as elk, bear, deer, and coyote. Richardson's son recalled that "nothing in the world surpassed the elk lard to grease a tortilla." The introduced cattle reduced the density of wildlife, but today it is coming back. The Marin Headlands are home now to deer, bobcat, grey fox, possum, raccoon, and rarely, mountain lion, drifting in from the north. There are jackrabbits, bush rabbits, meadow mice, deer mice, gopher snakes, garter snakes, and park rangers have heard reports of rattle snakes.

There used to be runs of steelhead salmon in the creeks, before they were dammed: Rodeo Valley, Tennessee Valley.

You might see a bobcat at any time of day or night, as they are what biologists call arhythmic — either nocturnal or diurnal. Or they may be crepuscular: active at twilight.

◇   ◇   ◇

On Rodeo Lagoon and nearshore ocean

115

 Sharpshin, a hawk commonly seen in fall migrations.

waters one may see the grebe and loon. Also, sooty shearwater, marbled godwit, sanderling, and willet. On lagoon, pond, and grassy lands, the great blue heron and snowy egret.

Ducks on the lagoon may be mallard, wigeon, pintail, shoveler, canvasback, scaup, bufflehead scoter, ruddy duck, as well as coot. And the brown pelican. On lagoon and rocky cliffs, terns and gulls.

Inland, in conifers, eucalyptus and willow thickets: the great horned owl.

Circling overhead: the aerial turkey vulture.

There are hummingbirds, swallows, flycatchers, kingfishers.

Jay and crow, bushtit and pipit, wren and wrentit, waxwing and kinglet, oriole and sparrow, bunting and blackbird, thrush and thrasher, creeper and raven, nuthatch and dove, tanager and finch.

Woodpecker, warbler, hawk.

All these may be seen, in different locations and at different seasons, in the Marin Headlands.

As early as 1900, when much of the land was military, members of the Golden Gate Audubon Society would come out to observe the birds and weather, to chat with the lighthouse keeper.

◆　◆　◆

● Tennessee Cove in the fog.

"THE last two decades have seen a revolution in our understanding of how the earth works. We now know that the crust and upper mantle of the earth, to depths of at least several hundred kilometers, are in circulating motion, much like the motion of water in a tea kettle. . . .

"Along certain narrow belts beneath the oceans, called spreading zones, hot material from deep within the earth rises to the surface to form new ocean floor; this new material moves away from the spreading zones to make room for still more ocean floor.

" . . . Dark basalt lava that is erupted onto the ocean floor through a crack that opens periodically along each segment of the spreading zone. . . .

"The most characteristic form [of this lava] is an accumulation of small bulbous masses called pillows. Cold seawater chills the lava as it erupts, forming a thin crust . . . of solid basaltic glass over a bulb of liquid lava. Lava continues to pour into the bulb, enlarging it and keeping the glassy crust broken along one or two continuously open cracks along which the surface of the bulb widens and chills to form additional glassy crust (a small-scale analog of seafloor spreading). The bulbous mass of lava is the pillow, with a convex upper surface. It is usually molded to the tops of older pillows and has a keel projecting downward along their junctions. . . . When the pillow reaches a meter or so in diameter, its surface grows so slowly that the crack freezes over and the pillow stops growing. The lava breaks out elsewhere to form a new pillow."

" . . . A bun- or biscuit-shaped mass . . . discreet blobs. . . . "

"In the sunlit surface waters of the sea, myriad minute, one-celled organisms secrete shells of lime (calcium carbonate) or of opal (a form of silica). When these organisms die, their shells sink slowly through the water, forming what Rachel Carson in *The Sea Around Us* called 'the long snowfall.' The lime-secreting organisms include foraminifera and various one-celled algae; those secreting opal include radiolarians and diatoms. Mixed with these minte shells is a fine mineral dust, usually red, blown form the desert areas of the continents.

"In most of the oceans the carbonate shells dissolve before they reach the ocean floor; the radiolarian shells remain and, together with the mineral dust, form the red radiolarian ooze of the deep ocean floors."

The basalt pillows erupted perhaps some two hundred million years ago, in the mid-Pacific, perhaps near what is now the Marquesas Islands. Overlain with the ooze of radiolarian chert and red shale — and with the pressure of new ocean floor forming at their backs — these rocks began their ponderous migration northeastward, to come to rest, finally — to dock — on the North American plate . . . to become, eventually, what is now called the Marin Headlands.

The headlands are a true *Allochthon*: "Masses of rock transported over great distance from their point of origin."

"As it converged with the continental plate, most of the oceanic crust, being the denser and heavier, plunged back into the mantle — that is, it was subducted. Floods of terrigenous sediment were poured onto the deep ocean floor from the continent or from volcanic island arcs above the subduction zone. Much of that sediment was derived ultimately by erosion from the land surface, and much of that sedimentary material, crushed, ground, and milled, with shiny slickensided surface, acted as the lubricant between the over-riding continental plate and the subducting oceanic crust. It remains today as an accretionary wedge, stacked against and beneath what was the leading edge of the continental plate. Embedded within that accretionary wedge are giant flakes of the uppermost basalt and overlying chert of the oceanic crust, the slabs of basalt and chert that make up the Marin Headlands, overlapping each other like shingles on a roof."

Although thought originally to have docked at their present location, it is now generally accepted that the Marin rocks accreted to the North American plate "to the south of here and moved to their present location by strike-slip motion along the continental margin. . . . " Such a motion — plates sliding past each other — creates a transform fault.

One final movement will account for the present Marin configuration: Subsequent to accretion, the headlands block — the entire stack — "has been rotated clockwise 90 degrees to 120 degrees about a vertical axis, possibly because of right-lateral shear along the San Andreas system. . . . "

"During the ice ages of the Pleistocene . . . the shoreline was on the other side of the Farallons, and San Francisco Bay was a dry valley. . . . When the glaciers melted, the sea rose to its present level, flooding San Francisco Bay and the lower ends of Rodeo and Tennessee Valleys, which first were narrow bays and are now lagoons. The broad flat valley floors, underlain by thick deposits of alluvium, are a product of this sea-level rise."

Subduction no longer occurs at the headlands, "and all one can see here are its products."

"Radiolarian chert underlies fifty percent or more of the headlands, and because of its resistance to weathering, makes up nearly all of the ridgetops and summits.

"Exposures along sea-cliffs and in roadcuts are continuous and magnificent."

But be careful. Some of the hills and shapes you see are not geological — they hide gun emplacements and ammunition dumps.

◇ ◇ ◇

● Pillow basalts: lava cooled under seawater.

Harold Gilliam writes:

"At the end of the last Ice Age, the great glaciers melted in such volume that the oceans overflowed. Over a period of thousands of years, rising seas flooded through the river-carved gorge at the Golden Gate and occupied an inland valley to create San Francisco Bay. . . .

"Thus the successive action of the river and the ocean created the only complete breach in the Coast Range, which borders the Pacific for most of California's length. As a result, the San Francisco Bay region is the meeting place of continental and oceanic air masses. Through the funnel of the Golden Gate and San Francisco Bay, the immense aerial forces of sea and land wage a continual war, and the tide of battle often flows back and forth. . . .

"Probably no comparable area on earth displays as many varieties of weather simultaneously as the region around San Francisco Bay."

" . . . There is actually no such thing as Bay Region climate. There are only innumerable microclimates varying widely from mountain to mountain, from valley to valley, and from point to point within the mountains and valleys."

"There are cycles within cycles, the ebb and flow, warm and chill. . . . "

"An ocean breeze laden with moisture and warmed by the spring sun during its long arc over the Pacific, strikes icy water which has welled up from the bottom nine hundred feet below. The air is cooled. . . . At the same time the same breeze scuffs the ocean beneath it into a ruffle of foam, flinging salt spray above the surface. As the ocean water falls back, the particles of salt remain in the air. Around a single air-borne salt particle a globule of the condensed water forms, large enough to be visible, small enough to float in mid-air.

"Millions of other salt particles are similarly flying into the air forming nuclei for drops of water condensed from the cooled wind. Inch by inch, mile by mile, as the wind blows over the cold surface, the droplets of water continue to form, creating first a hazy vapor, then a cloud on the water. The great summer fogs of the California coast have come into being.

"At the maximum the thick vapor forms a continuous bank perhaps a hundred miles wide, hundreds of feet high, and more than six hundred miles long. Slowly the white mass grows, rolls inland with wind, charges up coastal canyons in phalanx. . . .

"It is as if the ocean, impatient with the ponderous slowness of its own sea-level war on the cliffs at the continent's edge, were sending its aerial armadas to carry the attack inland. Along most of the six-hundred-mile front the fog is rebuffed by the coastal mountain wall. But at the Golden Gate, the one point in the coastline where the ocean itself has already breached the continental defenses, the air troops pour through with massive force, fanning out over the bay as if to exploit to the fullest the break-through in the enemy lines.

"Thus in the air as well as in the water the bay area is a main arena of battle between the elements. The gigantic land-sea conflict that gave birth to the bay is paralleled not only in the daily struggles between the flood and ebb of the bay itself but in the summer-long battle between the tides of the air as well. . . .

"So the war between the elements rages; the ocean sends its fog-bearing winds through the gap in the mountains to drive back the warm dry air and take possession of the land; the land air strikes back at the fog with withering blasts from the hot valley. And the ocean retaliates in force: The hotter the valley, the swifter the sea winds, the thicker the fog. . . .

"There is nothing on earth exactly like the fog of San Francisco Bay. None of the thousand evanescent forms of air and water that move across the globe between the equator and the poles is as fantastic in shape and motion yet as tangible and intimate as the thick white vapor that rolls through the Golden Gate in summertime like an airborne flood and spreads to the farthest reaches of the bay and its shores.

"In most parts of the earth, fog traditionally is a dark, disagreeable smudge that comes from nowhere, hides the sun, obscures the vision, afflicts the lungs, and casts a damp pall over the land. In San Francisco the fog is a thing of beauty and wonder. . . .

"Standing in the sun, you face a river of fog that may be a mile wide and hundreds of feet deep. Here the funneled winds whip through the narrow strait with accelerated speed and turbulence, and the fog, which elsewhere moves in at a rate of ten to twenty miles per hour, here seems to double its pace. In the course of an hour, a million tons of water vapor will float past in front of you. . . .

" . . . To plunge toward the bay, tumbling, eddying, and billowing like the spray of a mountain waterfall.

"In more than appearance these falls in the rivers of the air are like the falls in the rivers of the land. Both are composed of descending water; both send out clouds of mist and spray. . . .

● Folded chert, each millimeter taking roughly one thousand years to form.

"And so from March or April until early September the prevailing northwest winds whip down the California coast. . . . The rushing masses of air are so persistent and powerful that they are able to move even the surface of the sea itself. Driven before the spring and summer winds, the ocean surface runs south in a coastwise current one hundred miles wide.

"The turning of the earth affects not only the winds but everything that moves freely on its surface. Water, too, is subject to the same rightward drift that deflects the moving air, and the current running down the coast continually veers offshore. As the masses of water move away from the coast line, they tend to leave a vacuum; from somewhere must come more water to take their place. It comes from the only possible direction — straight down.

"The result is an overturn, an upwelling of bottom water from the continental shelf. From sunless depths several hundred to a thousand feet below the surface, water 'boils' to the top . . . the coldest water to be found in summer on any coast of the United States."

"As in most matched contests, the tide of battle flows back and forth with cyclical regularity. There is a daily cycle; the fog moves in over the bay in the afternoon, makes its greatest penetration at night, then retreats as the land air, heated by the morning sun, counterattacks in strength.

"There is a longer cycle, lasting from about three days to several weeks; its average length is about a week, however, and it can thus be termed a weekly cycle. Each night the fog penetrates a little farther than the night before and is driven back a shorter distance in the morning. Finally it reaches the Central Valley, becomes overextended and disappears. The bay then has clear weather for a few days until the weekly cycle begins again.

"And there is a seasonal cycle; from May to August, as the Central Valley heat increases and the sea winds through the Golden Gate grow to full strength, the hours of fog per day in San Francisco gradually increase. Then the winds and fogs begin to wane and the sun is seen more often until October, when the fog season ends."

"Sometimes in late September or October masses of moist air move north from subtropical Pacific areas off Mexico, bringing to the bay occasional high clouds, possibly showers, and, very rarely, thunderstorms. But usually even November is still calm and warm, with temperatures higher than in April. By this time, however, things are brewing far out over the North Pacific. . . .

"From off the deeps of the North Pacific, anywhere from the Hawaiian Islands to the Aleutians or the Gulf of Alaska, a low-pressure area of warm air is moving toward the California coast. Around it the winds are circling counterclockwise, blowing over the bay from the south. As the air masses of different temperatures meet, they give birth to clouds and to rain.

"The rain comes to the bay slowly, out of a dark gray sky. At first scarcely more than a fine mist, it envelops the hills, moves down to the shores, dampening docks and beaches, stippling the gray surface of the water."

"The rainfall pattern is more complicated than the fog pattern. The summer fog comes from the ocean and dissipates to the east, but the rain comes from several directions during the course of a storm. The most prolonged rains often form a family of storms following one another in rapid succession. . . . "

"At winter's end the spring sun, climbing farther north each day over the North American continent, brings welcome warmth to the land. . . .

"Slowly, through March and April and into May, the warming air over the land expands and rises; the weight of the atmosphere diminishes. . . .

"A thousand miles west of the continent's edge, however, the heaving blue waters of the Pacific respond far more slowly to the northward advance of the sun, and the air over the ocean remains wintry long after the continent has begun to warm. The cool, heavy air hugs the rolling surface and presses down on the water."

"The earth has completed another cycle around the sun; the coastal waters are beginning to well up from the bottom; and a long white arm of fog is once more moving silently through the Golden Gate. . . . "

"The war begins anew. . . . "

◆ ◆ ◆

● Wolf Ridge engulfed by Tennessee Valley fog.

Park Partners

When the army relinquished Fort Barry and Fort Cronkhite to the National Park Service, the service found itself in possession of over 200 structures in various stages of disrepair. A number of nonprofit organizations were invited to assist in restoring architecturally significant buildings, and in developing interpretive programs for the general public.

Following are brief descriptions of the seven current "park partners." They are listed alphabetically:

The California Marine Mammal Center rescues and rehabilitates sick or injured marine mammals that are stranded along the California coast. The goal is always to return the animal, healthy and wild, to its natural habitat. The center's hospital is open daily, free to the public. Ninety-five percent of the 350-person staff are volunteers. The focus on the humane treatment of animals serves as a bridge to promoting a wider environmental ethic. The center's education department offers a variety of programs for both children and adults. The center is located in a former Nike missile site, the missile storage area now filled with cartons of seal food, fish, and fish mash.

Headlands Center for the Arts has been given jurisdiction over several buildings in Fort Barry, buildings that are gradually being restored for use as artists' studios and residences, public meeting and performance space, and office space. The purpose of the center is to support artists in their exploration of the Marin Headlands and to make their interpretations accessible to the public. The center invites artists to live and work at Fort Barry; it also presents lectures, workshops, and performances, conducts symposia, and develops publications, of which this book is a major example.

The Headlands Institute was established in 1977, and its purposes are to extend the goals and philosophy of the National Park Service, offering environmental studies programs for students, adults, family groups, and teachers. The programs strive to impart a knowledge of science and nature and an appreciation of our connection with the environment. The institute's facilities consist of the Coastlab, furnished with scientific equipment, and specimens of the surrounding coastal life; the Discovery Room, where ecological concepts may be demonstrated with models; and the Conference Center, which includes a dining hall and dormitory-style bunk houses, with accommodations for up to 150 students. The Headlands Institute is a member of the Yosemite National Institutes established in 1971.

The Miwok Stables are located in a former dairy ranch that had already been partially converted for horses when the Park Service took over. The stables are now operated by the Miwok Valley Association, a nonprofit citizens group. A public riding program has been developed with organized trail rides and instruction by a private business with its own employees. Fees for trail rides, lessons, and boarding are approved by the Park Service. There is only one full-time employee of the association; the rest of the help is volunteer.

The Pacific Energy and Resources Center is a nonprofit public education, policy research, and conference center composed of natural resource and energy professionals and environmental educators. The center is committed to conserving energy and other natural resources, promoting sound resource stewardship and renewable resource alternatives, lessening the environmental impacts of resource production and use, and sharing its information and experience with policy makers and the general public. Water, air, energy, minerals, soil, forests, wildlife, people, and open space are all concerns of the center. Facilities include two public exhibit halls, the Children's Resource Lab, meeting and conference space, and a resources reference library.

The YMCA Point Bonita Outdoor and Conference Center offers meeting and conference facilities in a dramatic natural setting. The appeal is particularly to church, youth, or school groups, to environmental and civic/social organizations. Meeting rooms, dormitory, and cafeteria will accommodate up to 150 people.

The Youth Hostel is one of the busiest units of the approximately 300 such hostels across the United States. The location is in a building at Fort Barry that was originally used as bachelor officers' quarters, and it may also have been a secret communications center. The hostel will accommodate up to sixty-five guests at a time, and there is a three-day limit for each visit. This particular unit is self-supporting.

127

● Exploded shells and spent projectiles, October 1987.

General History

Angulo, J. de, and L. S. Freeland. "Miwok and Pomo Myths," *Journal of American Folklore* 41 (1928).

Anonymous. *The Bay of San Francisco*. Chicago: Lewis Publishing Co., 1892.

Anonymous. *Golden Gate National Recreation Area Guidebook*.

Anonymous. *Shark Point, High Point*. Mill Valley Historical Society, n.d.

Anthology. *Old Marin with Love*. Marin County American Revolution Bicentennial
  Commission, 1977.

Atherton, Gertrude. *California, an Intimate History*. New York: 1935.

Bancroft, Hubert H. *History of Alaska*.

———. *History of California*. San Francisco: 1894.

Beck, Warren A., and David A. Williams. *California*. New York: 1935.

Becker, Robert. "Disenos," *America West Magazine* (February 1967).

Blok, T., et al. *The Russians in California*. San Francisco: 1933.

Blount, Clinton M., and Dorothea J. Theodoratus. *Central California Indians*.
  Southwestern Museum Masterkey, 1985.

Brewer, William H. *Up and Down California in 1860–1864*. Berkeley:
  University of California Press, 1949.

Chartkoff, Joseph L., and Kerry Kona. *The Archeology of California*.
  Palo Alto: 1984.

Conrotto, Eugene L. *Miwok Means People*. Fresno Valley Publishers, 1973.

Fish, Allen and Maria Ferrara. *Hawkwatchers in the Fog*. The Pacific Raptor
  Report, Golden Gate National Park Association.
  San Francisco: 1987.

Fremont, John Charles. *Memoirs of My Life*. New York: 1887.

Geary, Ida. *Marin Trails*. Fairfax, Cal.: 1969.

Gudde, Edwin G. *California Place Names*.

Hart, John. *San Francisco's Wilderness Next Door*. San Rafael and London:
  1979.

Harte, Bret. *The Writings of Bret Harte*. 1872.

Khlebnikov, K. T. *Colonial Russian America*. Oregon Historical Society,
  Portland: 1976.

Kelly, Isabel. *Coast Miwok: Handbook of North American Indians*.
  Washington, D.C.: 1978.

Kelly, Isabel. "Some Coast Miwok Tales," *Journal of California Anthropology*
  5(1): 21–41.

Kinnaird, Lawrence. *History of the Golden Gate and its Headlands*.
  Manuscript, n.d.

Kotzebue, O. von. *A Voyage of Discovery into the South Seas*.

Lang, ? *The Indian and the Hispanic Heritage of a modern Urban Park*.
  Golden Gate National Recreation Area.

Lescohier, Ruth. *The Coast Miwok People*. Novato, Cal.: 1986.

Libertore, Karen. *The Complete Guide to the Golden Gate National
  Recreation Area*. San Francisco: 1982.

Margolin, Malcolm. *The Ohlone Way*. Berkeley: 1978.

Mason, Jack. *Early Marin*. Marin County Historical Society, 1983.

———. *The Making of Marin*. Inverness, Cal.: 1975.

Metcalf, Paul. *Apalache*. Berkeley: 1976.

———. *Firebird*. Minneapolis and Tucson: 1987.

Monroe-Fraser, J. P. *The History of Marin County, California*.
  San Francisco: 1800.

Olmstead, R. R. *Scenes of Wonder and Curiosity*. Berkeley: 1962.

Oral History Project of Mill Valley. Mill Valley Public Library, 1972.

Richardson, Steve. "The Days of the Dons." Manuscript, n.d.

Teather, Louise. *Place Names of Marin*. San Francisco: 1986.

Thompson, R. A. *Fort Ross*. Oakland: 1951.

Tracy, Jack. *Sausalito, Moments in Time*. Sausalito: 1983.

Wilson, Neill C. *Here is the Golden Gate*. New York: 1962.

Military History I and II

"The ABM Treaty and Interim Agreement
and Associated Protocol."
  Washington, D.C.: U.S. Government Printing Office, 1972.

Baring-Gould, S. *The Lives of the Saints*. London: 1877.

Chappell, Gordon. *Artillery Defenses of San Francisco Bay, 1794–1949*.
  Golden Gate National Recreation Area, 1981.

———. *Fort Cronkhite, California, and Battery Townsley, 1937–1973*.
  Golden Gate National Recreation Area, n.d.

———. *Forts Under the Sea*. Golden Gate National Recreation Area, n.d.

———. *Historic Fort Barry*. Golden Gate National Recreation Area, n.d.

———. *The Lime Point Military Reservation, 1850–1897*. Golden Gate
  National Recreation Area, n.d.

Killion, Tom. *Fortress Marin*. San Rafael and London: 1979.

Kinnaird, Lawrence. "History of the Golden Gate and its Headlands."
  Manuscript.

Lewis, Emanuel Raymond. *Seacoast Fortifications of the United States*.
  Washington, D.C.: Smithsonian Institution, 1970.

Peter, Joel. *The Nike Missile System*. Oakland: 1976.

Teather, Louise. *Place Names of Marin*. San Francisco: 1986.

Thompson, Erwin. *Forts Baker, Barry, Cronkhite of Golden Gate National
  Recreation Area*. Denver: National Park Service, 1979.

———. *Historic Resource Study, Seacoast Fortifications, San Francisco Harbor,
  Golden Gate National Recreation Area, California*. Denver:
  National Park Service, 1979.

Tracy, Jack. *Sausalito, Moments in Time*. Sausalito: 1983.

U.S. Army. *U.S. Army Nike in Defense of the Nation*.
Wilson, Neill C. *Here is the Golden Gate*. New York: 1962.

Shipwrecks

Delgado, James P. "Great Leviathon of the Pacific." Manuscript, 1985.
Delgado, James P., and Robert L. Bennett. *Research Design . . . Remains
   of the . . . Steamship Tennessee*. N.p., 1981.
Engel, Norma. *Three Beams of Light*. San Diego: 1986.
Point Bonita Times. Golden Gate National Park Association, n.d.
San Francisco Evening Bulletin, October 27, 1893.
Shanks, Ralph C., and Janetta Shanks. *Lighthouses of San Francisco Bay*.
   San Anselmo, Cal.: n.d.
Stocking, Fred M. *The Wreck of the S. S. Tennessee*. Golden Gate National
   Park Association, 1984.
Toogood, Anne C. *Lighthouses and Lifesaving Services*. National Park
   Service, n.d.
Wilson, Neill C. *Here is the Golden Gate*. New York: 1962.

Plants and Wildlife

Anonymous. *Golden Gate National Recreation Area Guidebook*.
Hart, John. *In Celebration*. Pacific Sun, 1982.
Howell, John Thomas. *Marin Flora*. Berkeley: University of California Press,
   1949.
McHoul, Lilian, and Celia Elke. *Wildflowers of Marin*. Fairfax, Cal.: 1979.
Nickerson, Roy. *Sea Otters*. San Francisco: 1984.
Orr, Robert T. *Marine Mammals of California*. Berkeley: 1972.
Woolfendon, John. *The California Sea Otter*. Pacific Grove, Cal.: 1985.

Geology and Weather

Gilliam, Harold. *San Francisco Bay*. Garden City, N.Y.: 1957.
—————. *Weather of the San Francisco Bay Region*. Berkeley:
   University of California Press, 1962.
Wahrhaftig, Clyde. *A Streetcar to Subduction, and Other Plate Tectonic
   Trips by Public Transport in San Francisco*. Washington, D.C.:
   American Geophysical Union, 1984.
—————. "Structure of the Marin Headlands Block, California: A Progress
   Report," *Franciscan Geology of Northern California,
   Pacific Section,* edited by M. C. Blake Jr. Los Angeles:
   Society of Economic Paleontologists and Mineralologists, 1984.
Wahrhaftig, Clyde, and Benita Murchey. *Marin Headlands, California*.
   Menlo Park, Cal.: U.S. Geological Survey, 1987.

LIST·OF·PHOTOGRAPHS

130

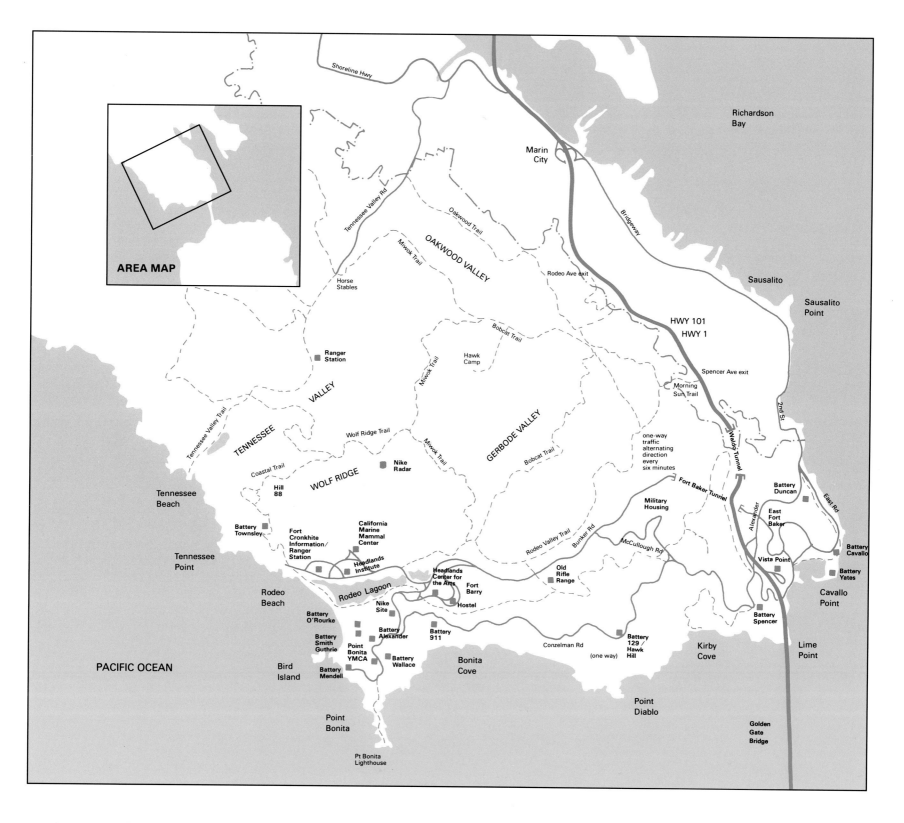

AREA MAP

133

Richardson
Bay

Marin
City

Sausalito

Sausalito
Point

Shoreline Hwy

Tennessee Valley Rd

Oakwood Trail

OAKWOOD VALLEY

Miwok Trail

Rodeo Ave exit

Bridgeway

HWY 101
HWY 1

Spencer Ave exit

2nd St

Horse
Stables

Ranger
Station

VALLEY

Bobcat Trail

Hawk
Camp

Miwok Trail

Morning
Sun Trail

Tennessee Valley Trail

TENNESSEE

Wolf Ridge Trail

Miwok Trail

GERBODE VALLEY

Bobcat Trail

one-way
traffic
alternating
direction
every
six minutes

Waldo Tunnel

Tennessee
Beach

Coastal Trail

Nike
Radar

WOLF RIDGE

Hill
88

Fort Baker Tunnel

Battery
Duncan

East Rd

Tennessee
Point

Battery
Townsley

Fort
Cronkhite
Information/
Ranger
Station

California
Marine
Mammal
Center

Military
Housing

Rodeo Valley Trail

Bunker Rd

McCullough Rd

Alexander

East
Fort
Baker

Battery
Cavallo

Headlands
Institute

Rodeo
Beach

Rodeo Lagoon

Headlands
Center for
the Arts

Fort
Barry

Old
Rifle
Range

Vista Point

Battery
Yates

Cavallo
Point

PACIFIC OCEAN

Battery
O'Rourke

Nike
Site

Battery
Alexander

Hostel

Battery
911

Battery
Spencer

Lime
Point

Bird
Island

Battery
Smith
Guthrie

Point
Bonita
YMCA

Battery
Wallace

Bonita
Cove

Conzelman Rd

(one way)

Battery
129 /
Hawk
Hill

Kirby
Cove

Battery
Mendell

Point
Bonita

Point
Diablo

Golden
Gate
Bridge

Pt Bonita
Lighthouse

Nº 14-B
Fort Cronkhite, Calif.
End of Roadway at Hill 417
Dec. 8, 1937

No 106-B
Battery Townsley
Fort Cronkhite, Calif
Form Construction
Walls Casemate No ?
June 29, 1938

Headlands: The Marin Coast at the Golden Gate was typeset by Miles DeCoster at Concert Typographers in Chicago. A variety of faces (Garamond, Palatino, Century, Optima, and Futura condensed) were employed to create typographic textures analogous to the subtle variations in the natural textures of the headlands and suggestive of the multitude of voices heard in the text. *Headlands* was printed on 80-lb. Quintessence Dull by Gardner Lithograph of Buena Park, California. The photographs are printed in black and gray using a 200-line screen. Roswell Bookbinding Co. of Phoenix bound the books. The typography, jacket, and binding were designed by Miles DeCoster.